Praise for *The Best American Poetry*

"Each year, a vivid snapshot of what a distinguished poet finds exciting, fresh, and memorable: and over the years, as good a comprehensive overview of contemporary poetry as there can be."

—Robert Pinsky

"*The Best American Poetry* series has become one of the mainstays of the poetry publication world. For each volume, a guest editor is enlisted to cull the collective output of large and small literary journals published that year to select seventy-five of the year's 'best' poems. The guest editor is also asked to write an introduction to the collection, and the anthologies would be indispensable for these essays alone; combined with [David] Lehman's 'state-of-poetry' forewords and the guest editors' introductions, these anthologies seem to capture the zeitgeist of the current attitudes in American poetry."

—Academy of American Poets

"A high volume of poetic greatness . . . in all of these volumes . . . there is brilliance, there is innovation, there are surprises."

—*The Villager*

"A year's worth of the very best!"

—*People*

"A preponderance of intelligent, straightforward poems."

—*Booklist*

"Certainly it attests to poetry's continuing vitality."

—*Publishers Weekly* (starred review)

"A 'best' anthology that really lives up to its title."

—*Chicago Tribune*

"An essential purchase."

—*The Washington Post*

"For the small community of American poets, *The Best American Poetry* is the *Michelin Guide*, the *Reader's Digest*, and the Prix Goncourt."

—*L'Observateur*

THE
BEST
AMERICAN
POETRY
2019

◇ ◇ ◇

Major Jackson, Editor

David Lehman, Series Editor

SCRIBNER POETRY

NEW YORK   LONDON   TORONTO   SYDNEY   NEW DELHI

Scribner Poetry
An Imprint of Simon & Schuster, Inc.
1230 Avenue of the Americas
New York, NY 10020

First Scribner edition September 2019

For information about special discounts for bulk purchases,
please contact Simon & Schuster Special Sales at 1-866-506-1949
or business@simonandschuster.com.

The Simon & Schuster Speakers Bureau can bring authors to your live event.
For more information or to book an event, contact the Simon & Schuster Speakers
Bureau at 1-866-248-3049 or visit our website at www.simonspeakers.com.

Manufactured in the United States of America

1   3   5   7   9   10   8   6   4   2

Library of Congress Control Number: 88644281

ISBN 978-1-9821-0656-0
ISBN 978-1-9821-0657-7 (pbk)
ISBN 978-1-9821-0658-4 (ebook)

CONTENTS

David Lehman was born in New York City. Educated at Stuyvesant High School and Columbia University, he spent two years as a Kellett Fellow at Clare College, Cambridge, and worked as Lionel Trilling's research assistant upon his return from England. His recent and forthcoming publications include *Playlist* (Pittsburgh, 2019), *One Hundred Autobiographies: A Memoir* (Cornell University Press, 2019), and *Poems in the Manner Of* (Scribner, 2017). He is the editor of *The Oxford Book of American Poetry* (2006) and *Great American Prose Poems: From Poe to the Present* (Scribner, 2003). *A Fine Romance: Jewish Songwriters, American Songs* (Schocken) won the Deems Taylor Award from the American Society of Composers, Authors, and Publishers (ASCAP) in 2010. He has also written books about murder mysteries, the case of Paul de Man, the New York School of poets, and Frank Sinatra. A contributing editor of *The American Scholar*, he edits the journal's weekly online feature "Next Line, Please." Lehman lives in New York City and in Ithaca, New York.

FOREWORD

by David Lehman

◇ ◇ ◇

In *The Unquiet Grave*, his book of *pensées* in the manner of Pascal, Cyril Connolly has a line that in its form may be the prose equivalent of a two-line imagist poem. "Poets arguing about modern poetry: jackals snarling over a dried-up well." Connolly wrote the line in 1945, but you can still hear that snarl today. Ubiquitous instruments of social media make it easy for anyone to pop off, get attention, air grievances, join the mob. While there is little enough criticism in the traditional sense, there is a tremendous amount of rage, and it fuels a censorious impulse that spells trouble for writers, publishers, believers in free speech, and readers of works that get denounced for one reason or another and then get pulled off the shelves.

The mob struck often in 2018. Certain radio stations, bowing to pressure, refused to air "Baby, It's Cold Outside," the classic duet and holiday favorite that won an Academy Award for Frank Loesser in 1949. Recorded by such redoubtable duos as Betty Carter and Ray Charles, Dinah Shore and Buddy Clark, Margaret Whiting and Johnny Mercer, the song is a long good-bye as on a balcony in Verona, only our Romeo begs for five minutes more and Juliet doesn't say yes and she doesn't say no.[1] The preceding sentence alludes to a play and two classic American popular songs for the reason that the predicament of girl fending off beseeching boy at the door is a show-biz tradition.[2] The offense: the song—courtly by the standards of some popular songs today—can be construed not as the clever repartee of a persistent suitor and an ambivalent lady, but as a melodrama in which the villain

---

1. For a more recent interpretation, see the song as performed by Chris Colfer and Darren Criss in the tenth episode of *Glee*'s second season.

2. "Five Minutes More" (Jule Styne and Sammy Cahn); "She Didn't Say Yes, She Didn't Say No" (Jerome Kern and Otto Harbach); the balcony in Verona: *Romeo and Juliet*.

will stop at nothing to take advantage of the damsel in distress. This is a nutty argument, reminiscent of the inattentive college student who somehow got the idea that *The Rime of the Ancient Mariner* describes a journey to a honey-sweet land of charm and romance.

The distinguished First Amendment attorney Floyd Abrams deplored what he called the "self-abasing decisions" made by important publications.[3] Three such stood out for him. *The New Yorker* invited Trump crony Steve Bannon to take part in a discussion, where you may be quite sure that he would have been raked over the coals by moderator and audience. But the magazine felt compelled to withdraw the invitation, because of Bannon's right-wing views. More grievous was the case of Ian Buruma, who lost his job as editor of *The New York Review of Books*, because he published a mediocre and arguably repellent article by a man with a history of sexual harassment. "Reflections from a Hashtag" by former CBC radio broadcaster Jian Ghomeshi reeked of puffed-up self-pity, but that's not what caused an outrage. What irked people was the very fact that the paper was giving a hearing to the disgraced broadcaster. Staffers grumbled that the decision to publish the piece was made against their wishes. Social media magnified the furor. "Now let it work," Mark Antony said after firing up the crowd in *Julius Caesar.* "Mischief, thou art afoot."

According to Buruma, a cabal of university presses, without whose advertising dollars the paper could not long survive, threatened a boycott. And the magazine that had once instructed readers on how to make a Molotov cocktail—the magazine that prided itself on printing fiery exchanges of in-your-face letters from angry readers and unrepentant writers—fired its top editor, a *New York Review* contributor since 1985. I was "convicted on Twitter," Buruma said.[4]

3. Floyd Abrams, *The Wall Street Journal*, September 29–30, 2018: "Retreating from, let alone abandoning the intellectual battlefield will only encourage more cries for self-censorship by offended readers. There is simply no excuse for these so often revered publications to comport themselves as if they resided in some sort of cultural re-education camp."

4. Interviewed in *Vrij Nederland*, Buruma said this of the *Review*'s publisher: "No, he did not fire me. But he made clear to me that university publishers, whose advertisements make publication of *The New York Review of Books* partly possible, were threatening a boycott. They are afraid of the reactions on the campuses, where this is an inflammatory topic. Because of this, I feel forced to resign—in fact it is a capitulation to social media and university presses." Conor Friedersdorf, "The Journalistic Implications of Ian Buruma's Resignation," *The Atlantic*, September 25, 2018. See also Lionel Shriver, "Easy Chair," *Harper's*, February 2019, pp. 5–7.

In midsummer 2018 a poem in the pages of *The Nation* spurred an angry backlash and a craven apology. "How To" by Anders Carlson-Wee used Black English for a monologue from an apparently homeless person asking for a handout. When it transpired that the author was white, a Twitter firestorm erupted in protest of the writer's appropriation of a black person's voice. The criticism, shrill and shaming, had its intended effect. The poetry coeditors of the magazine apologized, as did the author. So much for the tradition of editorial independence. So much for the habit of standing behind what you have published and welcoming letters to the editor in protest or support. Longtime *Nation* columnist Katha Pollitt voiced her dismay on Facebook: "So embarrassing! The poetry editors, Stephanie Burt and Carmen Gimenez Smith, liked the poem enough to publish it, which means they read it many times and did not see problems, but when challenged by the twitter mob they folded and sent themselves to reeducation camp. Now the whole magazine looks ridiculous. Thanks a lot!"

We who work on *The Best American Poetry* are familiar with such controversies. For all we know, it is possible that something in this edition of *The Best American Poetry* may raise hackles. We don't anticipate that, but even if we did, I like to think that we would stick to our guns as we offer the seventy-five poems that Major Jackson, our editor, has chosen as representative of the best poetry getting written today. I advocate making bold statements, offering no apologies, and leaving it up to others to mount arguments in favor of, or against, poems that are their own best defense.

★

Major Jackson is one of the foremost poets of his generation, and a natural choice to make the selections for *The Best American Poetry 2019*. As we headed into production, I asked Major how the experience affected him. "Most of my free time was spent reading to the 10th power," he said, balancing this activity with work on his own manuscript in progress, *The Absurd Man*. "I'd find myself tinkering on old poems (or yes, starting a new poem) after having imbibed on the verbal richness of others almost like having eaten a can of Popeye's spinach." In his own poems he felt pushed, he added, toward "great pockets of humor, if not a lyricism that hinted at the issues" facing us as a society. To the pessimists among us, Major has a succinct credo: "Poetry, like all art, never goes out of fashion. The will and spirit to represent our inner states and outer truth never dies. Humankind, as historians and scientists have observed, has continually sought new forms to reflect the changing shape of our existence. What waxes and wanes is our willingness to hear each other, to give each other a reading." To do that is exactly the mission of this book.

Pessimism is perennial. In September 2018, the poet Sally Ashton told me of a discovery she made in the stacks of the San José State University library: a 1926 anthology of American poetry in thirteen volumes edited by Edwin Markham, author of "The Man with the Hoe," a poem that achieved great popularity and raised the general awareness of the plight of laborers. Markham began his introduction to the anthology with these sentences that push back against the naysayers:

> Certain critics are saying that poetry is doomed to perish, to be sponged out by the hand of science. As well say that poetry will obliterate science, for each stands on its own ground, separate and secure, coequal, eternal, like Jungfrau and Matterhorn. Others, again, are saying that the world of poetry has been exhausted by the poets themselves—that nothing new is left to see or to say. But these, too, are idle words.

Substitute "technology" for "science" in this formulation and what remains is robust confidence. Do poets today have that confidence? Does the image of a great Alpine mountain, firmly fixed, with a wide base to accommodate the many and an apex to signify hierarchy, still apply to American poetry today? Has there been an abatement of the feeling that "nothing new is left to see or to say," or is "make it new" an imperative that now does more harm than good? And do people who believe that poetry is "doomed to perish" realize that this prediction is as worn and threadbare as it is?

★

As the editor of *The Best American Poetry 1989*, Donald Hall addressed these questions in his introduction, which appeared in *Harper's* bearing the headline "Death to the Death of Poetry." It may well be the single best riposte to the biannual magazine article predicting the demise of poetry and verse. Why, he asks, do so many people connected with poetry wonder whether we're fighting for a last cause? "The pursuit of failure and humiliation is part of it," Don wrote. But poetry, he added, is the victim of its surprise success. With the acceptance of creative writing as a popular part of the curriculum, more and more people write poems, some of these get published, and "ninety percent are doubtless terrible. (Shall we require capital punishment?) Because more poems than ever are written, doubtless more bad poems are written and printed. Amen."

Lionhearted Don died last year at the age of eighty-nine. He was a mentor and a model for me. A beloved professor at the University of Michigan, he gave up a coveted appointment (with tenure and all its perks) in exchange for a life of jeopardy, "forty joyous years of freelance writing," twenty of them shared with his late wife, the poet Jane Kenyon. In Eagle Pond Farm, in New Hampshire, Don, an inveterate correspondent, got so much mail—books, magazines, manuscripts, poems, and letters—that for a time the post office assigned him a zip code of his own. He made his living by his pen (literally; Don hired someone else to do his typing for him). He wrote about subjects not strictly literary, tried his hand at a variety of genres (children's literature, sports journalism), interviewed eminences, explored other arts (sculpture, painting), edited journals and anthologies, wrote textbooks.

Working with Don on *BAP 1989* was a wonderful experience—in their differing ways, he and John Ashbery taught me more than anyone else about editing a poetry anthology. Reading for the 1989 book, Don voted for pluralism over purism. In a sentence that I have taken to heart, he wrote that he forced himself "to admit some dead metaphors, maybe even an unscannable line in a metrical poem, and certainly a disgusting line break or two—for the famous sake of the whole . . . although I have wept salt tears over my principled antinomianism."

In 1994 Don asked me to succeed him as the general editor of the University of Michigan Press's Poets on Poetry series. As it was Don who invented the series, he and I were its only editors for its first thirty years. A denizen of New Hampshire, Don loved baseball in general, the Boston Red Sox in particular, so when it was my turn to toast him on the occasion of his seventieth birthday in 1998, I turned to the erstwhile national pastime, recalled that the Dodgers had exactly two managers for four decades, and grandly declared that the two of us were "the Walter Alston and Tommy Lasorda / of the University of Michigan Press, / and though you and I are not exactly like / either of them, Michigan links us / and we have uniform jackets to prove it."

Don won many accolades, book prizes, and medals, and was appointed the nation's poet laureate in 2006. "Poetry is my life," he wrote in *Essays after Eighty* (2014)—it was at the vital center of all his activities. He identified himself as a poet even before his student years at Phillips Exeter, Harvard, and Oxford. Some of the finest poems of Don's late period were chosen for *The Best American Poetry*:

"Prophecy," "History," "The Porcelain Couple," and "Her Garden" among them. With his versatility and energy, he always demonstrated the value of hard work in one's poetic practice. The title of *Life Work*, his 1993 memoir, sums up in two words the moral imperative that work represented for Hall. He revised incessantly, always believing that a better draft lay ahead. "Some of these essays took more than eighty drafts," he tells us in *Essays after Eighty*, a title with a concealed double meaning.

Provocative, fearless, Hall warned against the "Workshop Poem, McPoem, Clone-Poem, or Standard American Poem" in the 1980s, and surely we still suffer from the mass-produced "product of the workshop, a poem identically cooked from coast to coast." Aspiring poets who wish to write prose would do well to observe Don's strictures: "Don't begin paragraphs with 'I.'" "Avoid 'me' and 'my' when you can." "Do not commit dead metaphors." "Overuse or misuse of adjectives and adverbs makes prose weak and lethargic." "When we hope to persuade, we should pay court to the opposition."[5] In his essays he wrote what I call exclamation-point sentences, sentences next to which I place an exclamation point in the margin. In "Thank You Thank You," a 2012 *New Yorker* essay in which Don muses about the effect of poetry readings on the composition of verse, note in this sequence of sentences how cogent analysis and historical example give way to whimsy, humor, casual insight, and a totally unexpected opinion:

> Sound had always been my portal to poetry, but in the beginning sound was imagined through the eye. Gradually the out-loud mouth-juice of vowels, or mouth-chunk of consonants, gave body to poems in performances. Dylan Thomas showed the way. Charles Olson said that "form is never more than an extension of content."[6] Really, content is only an excuse for oral sex. The most erotic poem in English is *Paradise Lost*.

5. The first two of these quotations are from *Essays After Eighty* (Mariner Books), the third from *Breakfast Served Any Time All Day* (Michigan), the final two from the third edition of *Writing Well* (Little, Brown).

6. It was actually Robert Creeley who said that "form is never more than an extension of content." Don's was an easy mistake to make, as Creeley and Olson were close friends and colleagues; both were associated with Black Mountain College in the 1950s, and it was in their correspondence that Olson developed many of his theories on poetics.

It's hard to stop reading at this point, isn't it? Don's opinions were exemplary in the sense that they always made you think. And he had generosity of spirit; he felt, as I do, that the warring factions and movements of contemporary poetry can sit down and break bread together.

To the memory of Donald Hall we dedicate this volume in *The Best American Poetry* series.

Major Jackson was born in Philadelphia in 1968 and educated at Temple University and the University of Oregon. He is the author of five collections of poetry: *The Absurd Man* (W. W. Norton, 2020), *Roll Deep* (Norton, 2015), *Holding Company* (Norton, 2010), *Hoops* (Norton, 2006), and *Leaving Saturn* (University of Georgia Press, 2002), which won the Cave Canem Poetry Prize for a first book of poems. He is the editor of The Library of America's *Countee Cullen: Collected Poems* and *Renga for Obama: An Occasional Poem*. A recipient of fellowships from the Fine Arts Work Center in Provincetown, the Guggenheim Foundation, the National Endowment for the Arts, and the Radcliffe Institute for Advanced Study at Harvard University, Jackson has been awarded a Whiting Writers' Award and has been honored by the Pew Fellowship in the Arts and the Witter Bynner Foundation in conjunction with the Library of Congress. His work has appeared in multiple volumes of *The Best American Poetry*. Major lives in South Burlington, Vermont, where he is the Richard A. Dennis Professor of English and University Distinguished Professor at the University of Vermont. He serves as the poetry editor of the *Harvard Review*.

INTRODUCTION

by Major Jackson

◊   ◊   ◊

Does American poetry suffer from an abundance of "artistic dignity" and not enough "street credibility"? It's possible. When I asked a friend, a terrific prose writer, why she seems to have a slight disdain for poetry, she replied, "It's too elitist, like walking through a beautiful forest in which I know not where to look much less know what I am searching for. If I don't get it as a reader, then I feel like an idiot and somehow not worthy of the form." In years past, I would have fretted and dismissed her remarks as garden-variety philistinism, but my friend is admirably sensitive, a brilliant scholar, Ivy educated, and not someone prone to make trivializing remarks without great consideration.

Nor is she alone. For the better part of my life, at dinner parties, neighborhood gatherings, or the sidelines of my children's sporting events, I have had to confront the incredulity of ordinarily thoughtful, even erudite people who professed a similar antagonism toward poetry. An English department chair, a Renaissance scholar relishing a moment of candor with tapenade and a flute of Dom Ruinart in hand, admitted to me that he is "terrified" of poetry. The roots of such fears and anxieties have been the subject of many essays, and as a result there are as many defenses as there are quarrels with poetry, the most recent being Ben Lerner's humorous and insolently titled *The Hatred of Poetry*.

Three decades ago, my friend Sven Birkerts explained, almost prophetically, that poets write in an age of great distraction brought on by society's materialist compulsions and helplessness in the face of the latest seductive technology that render the inner musings of poets frivolous, irrelevant, and downright absurd. He writes:

> The race is busily standardizing itself and turning its attention outward; sciences, technologies, and the mass processing of information are the order of the day. Truth, for the time being, is what can be measured, calculated, or found on some instru-

ment. . . . And the *inner life* is given its due only when the strain of imbalance sends a crack zigzagging through the outer shell.

Around the same time, the late Polish poet Czesław Miłosz—who defined poetry as "the passionate pursuit of the Real"—pinpointed the source of the division to that moment in the nineteenth century when, just as the physical laws and equations of science began to assert themselves aggressively as the only relevant language to explain phenomena, poets with an eye on posterity (*Ars longa, vita brevis*) resolutely glorified the poem as "Art" for its own sake (*L'art pour L'art*) with no grander aims than to serve as a vehicle for their fame. The result? A weakening if not a loss of the poet's divine imagination through which humankind once profited from the ability to provide consoling metaphors that explained our passage from life to death. And thus, says Miłosz, the bond between the poet and the "great human family" ruptured, leaving us with no more than slim "volumes of poems incomprehensible to the public" amounting to a collection of "broken whisper[s] and dying laughter."

My faith in the transformative power of literature has never waned. However, a year ago, after a decade as the poetry editor of the *Harvard Review* and a score of years teaching undergraduates and graduate students, I began to share the sentiments expressed by my prose-writing friend, particularly regarding the preciousness of poetry. I became disenchanted with what amounted to beautiful architecture, glass fortresses of language whose walls and ceilings were lined with parallel facing mirrors in which the poet's ego or aggressive wit or moral superiority or mannered experimentation gradually faded into an abyss of itself, ad infinitum, and the age lost its witness, and the reader, yearning for human connection, was crowded out by a narcissism that was hard not to see. And these works were written by some of the best minds! If they failed, it was not for lack of talent. The poems worked for their intended audiences. They won prizes, adulation. Yet their lack of engagement with the world beyond art limits their appeal. It may even be that some poets, "afflicted with a modesty of ambition," as the recently departed Donald Hall declared, are apt to preen more for their Instagram feed than for Mount Parnassus.

When faced with the challenge of reading, I have sometimes found myself heavy bored, and the poem in question excessively underwhelming, lacking dimension or scale, or altogether devoid of any authentic feeling or thinking that might render the work illuminating or inspiring. About audience, I am fond of telling students that writing poetry is on par with composing for the gods who themselves are makers and, we are told, all-knowing, and that the challenge of any poet is to sing beyond the ennui and cynicism that are the byproduct of a restless omniscience. Even the gods are entitled to their revelations, a new purchase on their divinity.

Our art should do more than celebrate ourselves in Whitmanian fashion or sublimely frame our individualism or camouflage our moral shortcomings and desperate self-regard. Even the most personal poems should break through our novelistic sense of ourselves and stabilize the mutual fate of our shared destinies, our ephemerality.

On a December day, a Friday, as I was sinking into such dispirited, curmudgeonly feelings, an old friend from my youth in Philadelphia, the rapper Tariq Trotter aka Black Thought, sporting a tan fedora and tinted shades, dropped a ten-minute freestyle on Funkmaster Flex's radio show in the studios of Hot 97-FM (New York). It is a lyrical performance that has made the Philadelphia-born emcee a legend in hip-hop circles. With lines like "The microphone doctor, black Deepak Chopra / I'm a griot that make you wanna peacock your arm" and "I need royalty because I bleed royal / Go through the veins to the brain, fabulous and strange / My journalistic range is a catalyst for change," his flow, as we say, went viral and garnered a million YouTube views in a single day. By Monday morning, Jelani Cobb opined in *The New Yorker*: "In the combative, Darwinian world of hip-hop, [Black Thought's] densely arrayed metaphors, the calibrated poise, and casual displays of erudition ('I'm international—my passport pages are like *War and Peace*') all point to an artist who remains thoroughly in control of his gifts." That weekend I must have watched Black Thought's performance, ballooning into a cultural event, nearly a dozen times, and was reminded of what first drew me to poetry: verbal dexterity, a passionate intelligence, nutritional wit, all from a single imagination that sees beyond reality.

I had long ago put aside the highbrow argument that rap lyricists and songwriters such as Nobel laureate Bob Dylan are nonliterary, and thus I was open to the message that, although not a populist art, poetry has the potential of captivating more than an audience of one if it aims for the highest imaginative reaches of human speech, advances an untainted vision of humanity that preserves our dignity as a species, and works to maintain the sovereignty of language against abusive and corruptive rhetoric that breeds hatred—like much of what we experience today in our political sphere. Filled with this conviction, I calibrated my thinking about the project.

And thus editing *The Best American Poetry* came as a challenge to fulfill a single criterion: locate poems that by the sheer force and virtuosity of their making renew the bonds between reader and poet, the holy trinity of an art formulated once by Etheridge Knight as "The Poet, The Poem, The People." I sought poems that braved human connection; poems that battled the inertia of our daily routines and fixed modes of thinking; poems that shaded in the outlines of contemporary life and generously extended us into a profound understanding of ourselves as outraged, joyous, vulnerable, intelligent, loving; and finally, poems that overpowered the indifference we exhibit toward each other, which, if unchecked, may become one of the great horrors of living in the twenty-first century. Even with multiple social media platforms, even with satellites that televise from every corner of the world, we are, without art and literature, incapable of taking in the full width and complexity of our humanity and are likely to overlook the miracles that are found there. Now that our skies are once again our battlefields, we reflexively turn to our screens to see our proliferated differences, ideological or otherwise, amplified into profits, a kind of circus composed of codes.

What I am trying to say is that we are the forest, to take up my friend's metaphor: inscrutable, trodden, and, yes, beautiful. What we seek in poetry is ourselves beyond the inarticulateness, silence, and immeasurable mystery that define human existence. Poems work to free us of this tyranny. We are all aware of how difficult it is to absorb and embrace each other's unfathomable natures, let alone our idiosyncratic feelings and thoughts, which, when encountered in a poem, can make the uninitiated feel ruthlessly uncomfortable, to the point of bristling.

Still, how rewarding the happenstance when we encounter a poem that embodies that complexity and difficulty, the shape and contours of our deep humanity and aloneness, the words that give expression to what we feel or did not know we felt. Like *wow!* when one hears a jazz solo and a phrase is played amid the seeming chaos, wholly familiar, just slightly changed and *zoom!* it's off again navigating the suburbs and bedlam of sound.

Poems have reacquainted me with the spectacular spirit of the human, that which is fundamentally elusive to algorithms, artificial intelligence, behavioral science, and genetic research: *Sometimes I get up early and even my soul is wet* (Pablo Neruda, "Here I Love You"); *Earth's the right place for love: / I don't know where it's likely to go better* (Robert Frost, "Birches"); *I wonder what death tastes like. / Sometimes I toss the butterflies / Back into the air* (Yusef Komunyakaa, "Venus's Flytraps"); *The world / is flux, and light becomes what it touches* (Lisel Mueller, "Monet Refuses the Operation"); *We do not want them to have less. / But it is only natural that we should think we have not enough* (Gwendolyn Brooks, "Beverly Hills, Chicago"). Once, while in graduate school, reading Wordsworth's "Ode: Intimations of Immortality from Recollections of Early Childhood" in the corner of a café, I was surprised to find myself with brimming eyes, filled with unspeakable wonder and sadness at the veracity of his words: *Our birth is but a sleep and a forgetting: / The Soul that rises with us, our life's Star, / Hath had elsewhere its setting, / And cometh from afar.* Poetry, as the poet Edward Hirsch has written, "speaks out of a solitude to a solitude."

Are these the best poems? I count them among a growing personal anthology. For me, the best poems are those in which the author avoids concealment and obfuscation, and the truth of that person, eccentric, vulnerable, and brilliant, bears itself out in a sound heretofore unheard. The best poems evince such authenticity in language, form, thought, and emotion that leave us breathless, with the very air around us somehow changed. It's that moment when we stand mouths agape, hands above us in disbelief, at the courageousness, elegance, and purity of a magical utterance.

With the democratization of American poetry, we've lost a single, set measure by which to assess the "best" poems; our gains, however, include the multiple lenses through which we may perceive the ore lining the caves of the composing imagination. To our fortune, these lenses do not cancel each other out but force us to see more than a literary artifact that can be judged according to a strict code of appraisal. We are invited to exercise multiple consciousness, multiple literary and cultural traditions. The difficulty of the critic lies in the inability to shape-shift toward a greater incarnation of the human family that ultimately dwarfs one's tiny tools of evaluation.

All the poems in *The Best American Poetry 2019* afforded me a linguistic frisson that startled me to the recognition that what I seek from poems and art is substantive fellowship with humankind, proof we matter to each other. We cannot read each other's hearts, and sadly, silence is its own pervasive pastime. We are disposed more to assuming masks than we are to revealing the tenderness and freight within that might transform the world. More than any other time in history it seems the man and woman standing in close proximity to each other in a subway car are as far away from each other as two galaxies.

Maybe because of the divisions that partisan politics and manipulative rhetoric have wrought upon our country, maybe because we have yet to cultivate a citizenry that values the uniqueness and potential of *every* member of society, a good many of us yearn for the connections poetry promises. Whether as a mode of confession or a mode of inquiry, poetry grants significance to human life. If we are afforded the least amount of time during our day—as, say, at the Department of Motor Vehicles while waiting for our number to be called or just before a morning meeting at work—reading poetry yields the simple pleasure of language outside normal usage and the chance of encountering the stark voice of a sole individual on its way to blessed enlightenment. As an avenue into the inner life, poetry, including even the most radical language experiments, encourages us to experience each other in far richer and more meaningful ways than a news feed. Pound's old adage never tires: "Poetry is news that stays news."

Attribute all this to my democratic idealism, itself a product of having read so much Walt Whitman and Langston Hughes. By privileging and welcoming a wide array of voices, poetry inculcates a reverence for the vitality and diversity of the polis itself as experienced in the rhythm, cadence, and idiom of the age. Authentic uses of language, the kind we find in poems, rebuild our democracy and fortify it.

I undertook the task of editing *The Best American Poetry 2019* with an ardor and single-mindedness I reserve mostly for games of chess, discovering new restaurants, writing poetry, and foreign travel. What made me redouble my efforts was the fear that I may have failed to net a particularly extraordinary poem that appeared in print or online. I did not anticipate this kind of haunting worry, but it helped to drive me. Because I wished not to miss a single poem that would make the anthology even better than the last poem chosen, I carefully read, with deliberateness and resolve, thousands of poems in hundreds of online and print journals, newspapers, and magazines. Here, I must thank my family who, for a year, tolerated without complaint my irksome office confinement in the morning, after dinner, and during holidays, and glanced upon me as one who drives by a land surveyor peering through his theodolite.

Fortunately, I was not alone in my efforts. At times, David Lehman truly was my Virgil. He generously mailed poems that had the double effect of lessening my anxiety and strengthening my radar. For this, I thank him, but maybe even more, for agreeing to be included in this volume. Over three decades, David self-effacingly and politely declined previous editors' wishes to publish a poem of his in *The Best American Poetry*. His last appearance occurred in the debut volume edited by John Ashbery in 1988. "It Could Happen to You" is vintage Lehman: an homage to New York School poetry, the Mets, great literature, France, 1950s icon Rosemary Clooney, literary criticism, and ultimately, a celebration of his returning health.

The undertaking of editing *The Best American Poetry 2019* inaugurated a new commitment to the art. I found myself a champion of emerging poets, a celebrant of disremembered elder poets, and an advocate of those caught in between with several or more books that deserve a wide audience. Though I ventured forth with no *parti pris*, no agenda or preferred aesthetics, I gravitated to poems that electrified me to speechlessness and catalyzed my attention, leaving me seething with wonder at their monument to language and curiosity. To the dismay of my family, I sometimes woke in the middle of the night, and while pacing my upstairs hallway in the dark, recited the opening passages or ending lines to poems in this anthology.

The Best American Poetry 2019 might well be understood as a very public marker of my personal fluctuations of taste. Instinct plays a role in editing, just as it does in anyone's gastronomic preferences, and when it comes to poems I own up to my subjective choices. But the reading I did this year broadened my palate. The subconscious judgments congealing from my years as a teacher and editor gave way to an inclusive vision. In a wrongheaded mood I once proclaimed in an interview—where I often get in trouble—that we have, after the gains and experiments of late modernism and postmodernism, exhausted all that can be done inside a poem. How glad I am to have been proved incorrect. Plenty of the poems I read in the past year took as their mission an outright opposition to conventional poetics, often with great results—evidence that we need not fetishize avant-garde aesthetics as a thing of the past when it is a current that feels like a birthright at this point in the history of American poetry.

Auspiciously included here is the late singer Leonard Cohen, who made his first appearance in this series two years ago. Recently while watching the documentary *Ladies and Gentlemen . . . Mr. Leonard Cohen* with my son Romie, I came across early TV footage of the famed singer being interviewed with other writers, including the poet Irving Layton, on *The Pierre Berton Show*. At the time of the filming, 1964, a young Leonard Cohen was widely acknowledged in Canada as "the finest poet of his generation." On-screen, he was irreverent, brash, and cheeky. Berton appeared quite agitated at Cohen's unwillingness to answer straight a question about his care and concerns in the world as a poet. "Don't you care about anything? How can you be a poet and not care about something?" he exasperatedly asked. Leaning into the seriousness of the question, Cohen replied: "When I get up in the morning, my real concern is to discover whether or not I am in a state of grace." After his interlocutor confesses that he never really understood the phrase, Cohen goes on to explain: "A state of grace is that kind of balance with which you ride the chaos which you find around you. It's not a matter of resolving the chaos because there is something arrogant and warlike in putting the world in order."

If many of the poets assembled here would like to put the world in order, their poetry returns us to a state of grace by balancing this impulse with the demands of their art. The shadowy presence of our current political moment hangs over their work. Some refuse to turn away from the horrors of gun violence. Others add to the haunting tales of the #MeToo movement by coming to terms with historical wrongs owed to abuses of male power and narratives of gendered violence.

For some readers, American poetry begins with Whitman and Dickinson; for others, Anne Bradstreet holds that honor. For me, Phillis Wheatley inaugurates America's contribution to world poetry, for she is the first to "finger its jagged grain," expose the complexity of being an American and a casualty of its history of subjugation and plunder, the qualities which animate her poems.

The whole of last year I kept returning to the question: What does it profit a nation to uphold a national literature? Is this itself a kind of wall that delimits and determines who is American? Does "best" describe an articulation of poets whose work most signifies American-ness? I contemplated heavily these questions along with: What is American about American poetry? Does it mean we dream American dreams? Or possess American bodies? Maybe what defines us is our suppressed history or a need for psychic healing where art and poetry serve as a kind of rapprochement? Or is it our inalienable freedom to address aesthetic, political, and social concerns in our art without reprisal or fear?

I settled on the idea that despite our abstruse equivocations about the line between poetry and politics, poets today write in the wake of a long tradition of resistance in American poetry. They heed the ethical imperative to bear witness, to speak out, to advocate for social and economic equality, to combat the forces of various "-isms," yet not at the expense of artful language or a loyalty to the self—a duality of purpose that is consistent from generation to generation. In the most successful poems of witness, the lyric greatness we inherit is fully intact. As Martín Espada observes, poets who tackle issues such as sexuality, immigration, rampant technology, and anti-Semitism go beyond mere "protest to articulate an *artistry* of dissent." For all the worry about the homogenization of graduate creative writing programs and community workshops, we can take solace in knowing that the professionalization of poetry has not tamed the impulse of conscientious poets to put language to the service of righting injustices or vociferously claiming one's right to be heard.

With the many societal issues and challenges we face today, it is difficult at times for readers to hear the import of quieter poems. You'll find in these pages poems about love, the shock of aging, the consumptive spirit of desire, and the fear of hitting animals while driving at night. No less urgent, compelling, and aesthetically demanding, a strong thread of lyric poetry characterizes this volume. Many of the struggles, observations, and celebrations here are private, emotive, and affective.

Our education and reading practices have fully acquainted us with the orthodoxy of lyric poetry: a speaker who, in a state of rapture, disequilibrium, or acute possession, utters intense feelings and arrives, by poem's end, at some sacred cynosure of herself. Yet I found myself drawn to poems—some of them relatively long—in which the speaker seems discursively to work through questions of selfhood by addressing some existential dilemma that generously involves us in the drama and surge of its unfolding. The performance of the mind at work is one of the great pleasures of poetry and never more evident than on the surface of the poem that is imbued with an unassailable and visceral music.

Correspondingly, I listened intently to poems that reveal a distinctive American vernacular, unlike any heard before. The result? The poems in *The Best American Poetry 2019* represent a rich playlist of idioms and attempts at fastening the voice to the page. One hears the plaintive and melancholy as well as the ardent and fiery. One is likely to encounter the natural tendencies of unadorned, demotic speech as well as the eloquent propulsion of discursive, sculpted language. In all the poems, one realizes that the poets have come to terms with the imperative to refresh language so that its usage does not merely recycle clichéd beliefs that render us entombed in our aging mythologies, false histories, and unreliable memories. As Susan Sontag has written: "Language is the most impure, the most contaminated, the most exhausted of all the materials out of which art is made . . . It's scarcely possible for the artist to write a word (or render an image or make a gesture) that doesn't remind him of something already achieved." The poets gathered here assure us that poetry is not a dead technology, that we have not exhausted the potential for language to stir us and advance us toward greater epiphanies.

A number of cherished poets have died in the last year or so: Meena Alexander, Lucie Brock-Broido, Linda Gregg, Donald Hall, Tony Hoagland, Mary Oliver, Ntozake Shange, Derek Walcott. Mindful of their example, I have been consumed with the living and our sacred duty to remember the poets whose words have wrought our age to the effect that we can live with a little more decency, with a little more levity, a little more enlightened and wiser than before. This imperative I take to heart, for many of the poets who are passing from our lives have profoundly changed me; I have been "changed utterly" by their uncanny poems, guiding essays, fierce intellects, and literary citizenship. I fear the swiftness by which time, brutal critic that she is, grinds down their memories and the significance of their work. A few who were a continent in our imagination are reduced to a mere isthmus, a mere entry in the index of some academic textbook. It is painful to consider that their gifts might not trespass and survive into the next century with the same amount of force with which they have touched so many readers. The time will soon come, I hope, when we might lobby for a day in the United States to celebrate poets with a national holiday. Until then, we must teach and be engaged by the poems of the masters who have left us.

In my senior year of high school with plenty of turmoil at home defining much of my existence, I attempted to ease my anxieties by writing what I thought were poems in my book of rhymes. Even though I had friends who, like me, were melancholy and sui generis, and also wrote raps, I secreted away this book by covering it with a brown paper bag (something we public school students were required to do back then or our parents would be fined) so that it blended with my textbooks. I found poetry when I needed it. I could not fathom the decisions adults in my life made regarding their well-being and my safety. This is what brought me to the written word—this and the fact that, from a young age, I was enthralled by the mystery of existence. As a child, I thought an answer, a meaning, was just around the corner. Poetry allowed me, as a teenager, to participate in the making of that meaning.

Does the assertion still hold water that classrooms are where adults first learn to hate poetry? I wonder in how many classrooms across America right now some kid feels debilitated by the assignment to analyze a poem and is humiliated as a result. I know this is what happened to my prose-writing friend. In childhood, she and her brothers wrote poetry, an assignment given by their mother, who studied with Robert Hayden at Fisk University, to help pass the summer days. Her mom had them read the work out loud, to which she gave positive yet rigorous feedback. My friend treasured her mother's encouragement and the exchange of rhymes with her siblings. However, when she arrived in college, she encountered professors who predictably made the reading of poetry a chore akin to scrubbing the shower wall. For her, the interpretative act fetishized and eclipsed the pleasures of poetry; competing readings were rewarded or derided. She felt embarrassed and inept in the classroom; in her words, "not worthy of the form." The feeling of shame behind her abandonment of poetry probably holds true for many detractors of the art.

I want to remind the reader of *The Best American Poetry 2019* that far too many of us feel cornered when faced with the task of reading poetry. We feel compelled to reach irritably after fact and reason rather than to live and exist in the uncertainties, mysteries, and doubts, as John Keats would have us do. Poems are works of art, not necessarily meaning-making machines meant to be reverse-engineered. As someone who has assigned and taught previous editions of *The Best American Poetry*, I hope that teachers of this volume instruct students how to experience language and its designs, to embrace what reaches them *and* what eludes them, to accept and exist in that space of wonder and mystery. Mastery over a poem is a fiction and should be discouraged; but the skills drawn from discerning the nuances of speech and sensitivities of form are manifold. Moreover, I'll go out on a limb here and say that the space of confusion students complain about ("I don't get it") can itself be inspirational and freeing.

My high school English teacher at Central High School in Philadelphia, Mr. Plummer, was a man of immense affect with an exaggerated mustache that, depending on your TV habits, put you in mind of period actors Billy Dee Williams or Burt Reynolds. He primarily taught Shakespeare; I still have my copy of *The Merchant of Venice* from his class. He came alive reading any number of Shakespeare's sonnets, but he saved his best performances for Robert Frost. He'd recite "Nothing Gold Can Stay" and "Birches" with great enthusiasm.

Mr. Plummer would begin classes the first Monday of the month while calling roll by asking each student if he or she were ignorant—a question to which each of us would have to reply with these exact words, "Yes Mr. Plummer; I am ignorant." He worked as a high school teacher long enough to convince the school district to grant him a comfortable chair at his desk and a tea station that he kept stocked with fresh boxes of Lorna Doones. After downshifting his recliner into a restful position, he would lounge and, while sipping from a steaming cup of Earl Grey, call each of us by name beginning with the first row. "Mister Jeffrey Arons, are you ignorant?" "Yes Mr. Plummer, I am ignorant." The whole routine was entertaining. He seemed increasingly to beam from inside with each admission, which to many of us felt like a public shaming.

Once, one morning, after I petulantly replied "No, Mr. Plummer, I am not ignorant," he took a bite from his cookie, set the other half on the saucer, and walked over to my desk in the second row and dramatically pronounced: "Everyone! Mr. Jackson has the whole of human knowledge inside his large globular noggin." He then proceeded to squeeze—for what felt like a long time—my head while he lectured on the ancient philosopher Socrates and the virtues of ignorance, a pedagogical moment that today could land him in court.

On another occasion, when I accidentally handed in my book of poems, mistaking it for my textbook, Mr. Plummer looked down at me, then read silently one of my poems. I was terrified at what was to come next. To my surprise, he announced to my friends that indeed I was a poet and asked if he could recite what he had just read silently to himself, which he said was slightly impenetrable but fulfilling in its strangeness. I do not remember the poem, only his mouthing the words with deep relish as if they were his own, a transaction to which I would become addicted. He became a champion, someone whose readings and valuing of poems would partially dictate my path in life.

With *The Best American Poetry 2019* I wish to pay homage to all teachers who inspire their students to find sustenance from poetry. I also want to acknowledge the inimitable Alice Quinn, who announced during my long year of reading that she was stepping down as executive director of the Poetry Society of America. In her work there and at *The New Yorker*, Alice displayed a vision of and service to the art, and helped not only to widen audiences through innovative programming but also to aid in the growth and development of many young poets, including yours truly. She approached her protean duties like a true impresario. If we are in the throes of a great age for poetry, it is to such stewards of our literature that we owe our thanks. In their honor, enjoy the poems in *The Best American Poetry 2019*.

THE
BEST
AMERICAN
POETRY
2019

Phase One

◇ ◇ ◇

For leaving the fridge open
last night, I forgive you.
For conjuring white curtains
instead of living your life.

For the seedlings that wilt, now,
in tiny pots, I forgive you.
For saying *no* first
but *yes* as an afterthought.

I forgive you for hideous visions
after childbirth, brought on by loss
of sleep. And when the baby woke
repeatedly, for shouting silently

in the dark, "What's your beef?"
I forgive your letting vines
overtake the garden. For fearing
your own propensity to love.

For losing, again, your bag
en route from San Francisco;
for the equally heedless drive back
on the caffeine-fueled return.

I forgive you for leaving
windows open in rain
and soaking library books
again. For putting forth

only revisions of yourself,
with punctuation worked over,
instead of the disordered truth,
I forgive you. For singing mostly

when the shower drowns
your voice. For so admiring
the drummer you failed to hear
the drum. In forgotten tin cans,

may forgiveness gather. Pooling
in gutters. Gushing from pipes.
A great steady rain of olives
from branches, relieved

of cruelty and petty meanness.
With it, a flurry of wings, thirteen
gray pigeons. Ointment reserved
for healers and prophets. I forgive you.

I forgive you. For feeling awkward
and nervous without reason.
For bearing Keats's empty vessel
with such calm you worried

you had, perhaps, no moral
center at all. For treating your mother
with contempt when she deserved
compassion. I forgive you. I forgive

you. I forgive you. For growing
a capacity for love that is great
but matched only, perhaps,
by your loneliness. For being unable

to forgive yourself first so you
could then forgive others and
at last find a way to become
the love that you want in this world.

from *Asian American Literary Review*

ROSA ALCALÁ

You & the Raw Bullets

◇ ◇ ◇

Why the image just now of a bullet entering the mouth? Why call it
raw, when it isn't sticky and pink like a turkey meatball, just the usual:
gold, and shiny, and cylindrical? What about this bullet is uncooked?
Why does it multiply with you in parka or short skirt, versions of
the you that you were, swallowing raw bullets as you walked? The
images come without assailant, without gun, just the holes the bullets
opened, the holes through which they went. And now at the age in
which you ride enclosed in glass like the Pope or President you are
spitting up the bullets slow-simmered in your own juices. You are
shitting them out, feeling them drop from you in clumps of blood,
in the days of bleeding left. But you cannot expel all of them. Some,
raw as the day they entered, have expanded their mushroom heads
into the flesh, or lodged their hot tip into the taste center of the brain.
Will the tongue's first encounter with pomegranate seeds be forever
a lost Eden, that fruit of your girlhood, which, also meaning grenade,
was perhaps never innocent? Do your own raw bullets come back to
you, my friends? Let us legislate the active voice, instead. Not, "Many
bodies have been used as blanks, aluminum cans." But, "Here are the
men who pulled the trigger, look at them."

from Poem-a-Day

Update on Werewolves

◊　◊　◊

In the old days, all werewolves were male.
They burst through their bluejean clothing
as well as their own split skins,
exposed themselves in parks,
howled at the moonshine.
Those things frat boys do.

Went too far with the pigtail yanking—
growled down into the pink and wriggling
females, who cried *Wee wee*
wee all the way to the bone.
Heck, it was only flirting,
plus a canid sense of fun:
See Jane run!

But now it's different:
No longer gender specific.
Now it's a global threat.

Long-legged women sprint through ravines
in furry warmups, a pack of kinky
models in sado-French *Vogue* getups
and airbrushed short-term memories,
bent on no-penalties rampage.

Look at their red-rimmed paws!
Look at their gnashing eyeballs!
Look at the backlit gauze
of their full-moon subversive halos!

Hairy all over, this belle dame,
and it's not a sweater.

O freedom, freedom and power!
they sing as they lope over bridges,
bums to the wind, ripping out throats
on footpaths, pissing off brokers.

Tomorrow they'll be back
in their middle-management black
and Jimmy Choos
with hours they can't account for
and first dates' blood on the stairs.

They'll make some calls: *Good-bye.*
It isn't you, it's me. I can't say why.
They'll dream of sprouting tails
at sales meetings,
right in the audiovisuals.
They'll have addictive hangovers
and ruined nails.

from *Freeman's*

Central Park

◇ ◇ ◇

I'd like to buy one when I die,
one of the benches not yet spoken for,
not yet tagged with a small stainless plaque

and someone else's name.
If they're all gone, please
help me carry a replica

to the boat pond so I can sit
and watch the model boats get nowhere
beautifully, rented by the fixed hours

I'm grateful not to be out of yet.
Another flicker of love,
an updated Triple-A membership,

and a handful of Pilot G-Tec-C4 blue-black pens,
what else do I need?
Universe,

watch over us.
Boat, my poor faraway father says,
as if my mother has never seen one.

Boat, he says, and we say, Yes,
aren't they beautiful.
Come winter,

the boathouse here is locked up,
the pond drained,
except one year it wasn't

and my son and I convinced ourselves
his new Golden Bright
could sail across.

Merry Christmas, no one said
as I pulled the black plastic liner bags
from the empty trash cans

and stepped into them,
one for each leg,
and waded into the addled water

to salvage the present.
I think that moment is something to remember,
or something to remember me by,

brief, vivid, foolhardy—
even the revenants watching from the line of benches
said so:

thus have been our travels.
Oblivion, they said,
there's no unenduring it.

from *The American Poetry Review*

America Will Be

◇ ◇ ◇

after Langston Hughes

I am now at the age where my father calls me brother
when we say goodbye. *Take care of yourself, brother,*
he whispers a half beat before we hang up the phone,
and it is as if some great bridge has unfolded over the air
between us. He is 68 years old. He was born in the throat
of Jim Crow Alabama, one of ten children, their bodies side
by side in the kitchen each morning like a pair of hands
exalting. Over breakfast, I ask him to tell me the hardest thing
about going to school back then, expecting some history
I have already memorized. Boycotts & attack dogs, fire
hoses, Bull Connor in his personal tank, candy paint
shining white as a slaver's ghost. He says: *Having to read
The Canterbury Tales.* He says: *eating lunch alone.* Now, I hear
the word *America* & think first of my father's loneliness,
the hands holding the pens that stabbed him as he walked
through the hallway, unclenched palms settling
onto a wooden desk, taking notes, trying to pretend
the shame didn't feel like an inheritance. You say *democracy*
& I see the men holding documents that sent him off
to war a year later, Motown blaring from a country
boy's bunker as napalm scarred the sky into jigsaw
patterns, his eyes open wide as the blooming blue
heart of the lightbulb in a Crown Heights basement where he
& my mother will dance for the first time, their bodies
swaying like rockets in the impossible dark & yes I know
that this is more than likely not what you mean
when you sing *liberty* but it is the only kind

I know or can readily claim, the times where those hunted
by history are underground & somehow daring to love
what they cannot hold or fully fathom when the stranger
is not a threat but the promise of a different ending
I woke up this morning and there were men on television
lauding a wall big enough to box out an entire world,
families torn with the stroke of a pen, citizenship
little more than some garment that can be stolen or reduced
to cinder at a tyrant's whim my father knows this grew up
knowing this witnessed firsthand the firebombs
the Klan multiple messiahs love soaked & shot through
somehow still believes in this grand bloodstained
experiment still votes still prays that his children might
make a life unlike any he has ever seen. He looks
at me like the promise of another cosmos and I never
know what to tell him. All of the books in my head
have made me cynical and distant, but there's a choir
in him that calls me forward my disbelief built as it is
from the bricks of his belief not in any America
you might see on network news or hear heralded
before a football game but in the quiet
power of Sam Cooke singing that he was born
by a river that remains unnamed that he runs
alongside to this day, some vast and future country
some nation within a nation, black as candor,
loud as the sound of my father's
unfettered laughter over cheese eggs & coffee
his eyes shut tight as armories his fists
unclenched as if he were invincible

from *The Nation*

Afternoons at the Lake

◊　◊　◊

I would rather be trapped in an attic with rats than play Monopoly
all the afternoons it takes to lose the last of my money to the already

super-rich one-percent grandchild, to line up cheap green houses
on my low-rent Baltic and Mediterranean Avenues in a futile attempt

to collect enough to survive the next round of rent on Boardwalk
or Park Place, to feel pitiful gratitude when I Receive for Services

twenty-five dollars. Everything will be gone, save the smallest
denominations, the Asian crayfish will overrun the native,

the Autumn Olive will proliferate, the tallest thing will grow taller,
will be layered with gold, will turn to gold, will harden its gold heart.

It will squander, jet, pocket, dole, win past wanting to win, dig
the mineshaft, the ore, eat up the hillside the birds the whales,

crack the foundations of houses, force the defaulters into the street.
Dice will land as they will, will cause the tiny car to bounce

happily from St. James Place to Indiana Avenue, a galaxy of gobble,
will enable the placement of flamboyant hotels on the coast

where waters wash with exquisite music shoreward, all of it owned
by the God who dwells inside the winning, who has not said

otherwise yet, who owns Free Parking and Jail, who owns the treeless
board the classy neighborhoods as well as the ones with the rats

and smashed-out windows, the murderous scrawl of languages
on walls, the smiling God holding the center with top hat and cane,

as I at last step out on the dock with my coffee and say to myself
the lines where Keats rhymes "think" with "nothingness do sink."

from *The Southern Review*

Essay on Joy

◊ ◊ ◊

When as a child my father deemed my weight excessive, the measure of which shifted according to whim, he would take his underwear off of his body and place it on top of my head. I was to run in circles around the house, wearing it, for a prescribed number of times. This was called "exercise."

I am undertaking a new labor: I will imagine myself into deep, focused, and strange hatreds. Spinoza writes, *He who imagines that what he hates is destroyed will rejoice.* Some years ago, dozens of grackles fell dead from the sky in Boston, the cause unknown. And so I think: *I detest grackles.* I rejoice.

If asked, I would have explained the cause: somewhere in a level of atmosphere for which humans hold no keys lived a green-shining carrion crow. As her name indicates, she ate dead bodies. But nothing had died there, ever; and so, she was hungry. She was kept company by this lack.

Sometimes, I tell myself that I cannot think of a lover with terribly much feeling at all. But this is a lie. The absence of feeling is an assertion of a feeling, and it is a memory, or an *exercise*, of a kind of a joy I sometimes fear I have forgotten, because, as a lover, I have been slighted, and, as a child, often betrayed.

For some length of time that a crow considers painful and I cannot measure, she caressed her lack like a lover. But then she came to fear her lover, for it caused her pain, and she could not convince herself that she had no feeling for her lover. So she undertook an exercise of destruction and began to kill.

When as a child I turned to violence, my mother, who also feared my father and even more feared the thought that I might become him, tried to warn, *A fist is always made with four fingers that point back toward you.* This is the kind of thing a grackle would say, because on their feet is one toe that always points backward.

Then the crow's fallow field of carrion was her new creation, and she had grown accustomed to hating the products of her own making. She ate some, and so she finally grew in size, and hated that, too. *She who imagines what she hates is destroyed will rejoice.* She opened a hole in the bottom of the atmosphere. Her kills fell.

from *The Rumpus*

Six Obits

◇ ◇ ◇

Friendships—died June 24,
2009, once beloved but not
consistently beloved. The mirror
won the battle. I am now
imprisoned in the mirror. All my
selves spread out like a deck of
cards. It's true, the grieving
speak a different language. I am
separated from my friends by
gauze. I will drive myself to my
own house for the party. I will
make small talk with myself,
spill a drink on myself. When
it's over, I will drive myself back
to my own house. My
conversations with other parents
about children pass me on the
staircase on the way up and
repeat on the way down. Before
my mother's death, I sat
anywhere. Now I look for the
image of the empty chair near the
image of the empty table. An
image is a kind of distance. An
image of me sits down.
Depression is a glove over the
heart. Depression is an image of
a glove over the image of a heart.

Optimism—died on August 3, 2015, a slow death into a pavement. At what point does a raindrop accept its falling? The moment the cloud begins to buckle under it or the moment the ground pierces it and breaks its shape? In December, my mother had her helper prepare a Chinese hot pot feast. My mother said it would probably be her last Christmas. I laughed at her. She yelled at my father all night. I put a fish ball in my mouth. My optimism covered the whole ball as if the fish had never died, had never been gutted and rolled into a humiliating shape. To acknowledge death is to acknowledge that we must take another shape.

Affection—died on November 12, 1978, the last picture I see of my mother's arms around me. At the funeral, I never touched my sister. When the room was finally empty, she sat in the front row with her spouse. I watched his arm lift and fall onto her shoulder. When my spouse's parents died, both times, he burst into tears, inextinguishable tears that quickly extinguished. The first time, he hugged me and not his family. The second time, he hugged no one. When the nurse called, she said, *I'm sorry, but your mother passed away this morning.* When I told my children, the three of us hugged in a circle, burst *into* tears. As if the tears were already there crying on their own and we, the newly bereaved, exploded into them. In the returning out of the tears, the first person *I* dissolves a little more each time.

Clothes—died on August 10, 2015. We stuffed them into lawn bags to donate. Shirt after shirt, button-down after button-down, dress after dress, limb after limb. A few leapt out to me like the flame from a nightmare, the kind of flame that almost seems human in its gestures. I kept those. I kept the hundreds of pencils. I am writing with a pencil from my mother's drawer. It says *Detroit Public Schools*, where she taught. Each sentence fights me. Once we rolled her downstairs, played croquet and putt putt golf. She sat and watched, her vacant eyes not seeing anything we saw. As if she were looking beyond us, beyond the sun. The days of August already made a certain way that she could see and we couldn't. I left her in the sun too long. One child doing cartwheels on the grass as my mother looked on, wearing the white blouse with the small pink flowers swirling in a pattern. I kept the stare. I kept the flowers. And I donated the vacant shirt.

The Ocean—died on August 21, 2017, when I didn't jump from the ship. Instead, I dragged the door shut and pulled up the safety latch. The water in my body wanted to pour into the ocean and I imagined myself being washed by the water, my body separating into the droplets it always was. I could feel the salt on my neck for days. A woman I once knew leapt out of a window to her death. The difference was she was being chased. Some scientists say the ocean is warming. Some say the ocean has hypoxic areas with no oxygen. Even water has hierarchy. A child's death is worse than a woman's death unless the woman who died was the mother of the child and the only parent. If the woman who died was the mother of an adult, it is merely *a part of life.* If both mother and daughter die together, it is *a shame.* If a whole family dies, it is a *catastrophe.* What will we call a whole ocean's death? *Peace.*

The Clock—died on June 24, 2009, and it was untimely. How many times my father has failed the *clock test*. Once I heard a scientist with Alzheimer's on the radio, trying to figure out why he could no longer draw a clock. It had to do with the *superposition of three types*. The hours represented by 1–12, the minutes where a 1 no longer represents 1 but a 5, and a 2 now represents 10, then the second hand that measures 1 to 60. I sat at the stoplight and thought of the clock, its perfect circle and its *superpositions,* all the layers of complication on a plane of thought, yet the healthy read the clock in one single instant without a second thought. I think about my father and his lack of first thoughts, how every thought is a second or third or fourth thought, unable to locate the first most important thought. I wonder about the man on the radio and how far his brain has degenerated since. Marvel at how far our brains allow language to wander without looking back but knowing where the pier is. If you unfold an origami swan, and flatten the paper, is the paper sad because it has seen the shape of the swan or does it aspire towards flatness, a life without creases? My father is the paper. He remembers the swan but can't name it. He no

longer knows the paper swan
represents an animal swan. His
brain is the water the animal
swan once swam in, holds
everything, but when thawed, all
the fish disappear. Most of the
words we say have something to
do with fish. And when they're
gone, they're gone.

from *The Kenyon Review*

I Invite My Parents to a Dinner Party

◇　◇　◇

In the invitation, I tell them for the seventeenth time
(the fourth in writing), that I am gay.

In the invitation, I include a picture of my boyfriend
& write, *You've met him two times. But this time,*

you will ask him things other than can you pass the
whatever. You will ask him

about him. You will enjoy dinner. You will be
enjoyable. Please RSVP.

They RSVP. They come.
They sit at the table & ask my boyfriend

the first of the conversation starters I slip them
upon arrival: *How is work going?*

I'm like the kid in *Home Alone*, orchestrating
every movement of a proper family, as if a pair

of scary yet deeply incompetent burglars
is watching from the outside.

My boyfriend responds in his chipper way.
I pass my father a bowl of fish ball soup—*So comforting,*

isn't it? My mother smiles her best
Sitting with Her Son's Boyfriend

Who Is a Boy Smile. I smile my Hurray for Doing
a Little Better Smile.

Everyone eats soup.
Then, my mother turns

to me, whispers in Mandarin, *Is he coming with you
for Thanksgiving? My good friend is & she wouldn't like*

this. I'm like the kid in *Home Alone*, pulling
on the string that makes my cardboard mother

more motherly, except she is
not cardboard, she is

already, exceedingly my mother. Waiting
for my answer.

While my father opens up
a *Boston Globe*, when the invitation

clearly stated: *No security
blankets.* I'm like the kid

in *Home Alone*, except the home
is my apartment, & I'm much older, & not alone,

& not the one who needs
to learn, has to—*Remind me*

what's in that recipe again, my boyfriend says
to my mother, as though they have always, easily

talked. As though no one has told him
many times, what a nonlinear slapstick meets

slasher flick meets psychological
pit he is now co-starring in.

Remind me, he says
to our family.

from Poem-a-Day

Drank a Lot

◇ ◇ ◇

i drank a lot. i lost my job.
i lived like nothing mattered.
then you stopped, and came across
my little bridge of fallen answers.

i don't recall what happened next.
i kept you at a distance.
but tangled in the knot of sex
my punishment was lifted.

and lifted on a single breath—
no coming and no going—
o G-d, you are the only friend
i never thought of knowing.

your remedies beneath my hand
your fingers in my hair
the kisses on our lips began
that ended everywhere.

and now our sins are all confessed
our strategies forgiven
it's written that the law must rest
before the law is written.

and not because of what i'd lost
and not for what i'd mastered
you stopped for me, and came across
the bridge of fallen answers.

tho' mercy has no point of view
and no one's here to suffer
we cry aloud, as humans do:
we cry to one another.

And now it's one, and now it's two,
And now the whole disaster.
We cry for help, as humans do—
Before the truth, and after.

And Every Guiding Light Was Gone
And Every Teacher Lying—
There Was No Truth In Moving On—
There Was No Truth In Dying.

And Then The Night Commanded Me
To Enter In Her Side—
And Be As Adam Was To Eve
Before The Great Divide.

her remedies beneath my hand
her fingers in my hair—
and every mouth of hunger glad—
and deeply unaware.

and here i cannot lift a hand
to trace the lines of beauty,
but lines are traced, and beauty's glad
to come and go so freely.

and from the wall a grazing wind,
weightless and routine—
it wounds us as i part your lips
it wounds us in between.

and every guiding light was gone
and every sweet direction—
the book of love i read was wrong
it had a happy ending.

And Now There Is No Point Of View—
And Now There Is No Other—
We Spread And Drown As Lilies Do—
We Spread And Drown Forever.

You are my tongue, you are my eye,
My coming and my going.
O G-d, you let your sailor die
So he could be the ocean.

And when I'm at my hungriest
She takes away my tongue
And holds me here where hungers rest
Before the world is born.

And fastened here we cannot move
We cannot move forever
We spread and drown as lilies do—
From nowhere to the center.

Escaping through a secret gate
I made it to the border
And call it luck—or call it fate—
I left my house in order.

And now there is no point of view—
And now there is no other—
We spread and drown as lilies do—
We spread and drown forever.

Disguised as one who lived in peace
I made it to the border
Though every atom of my heart
Was burning with desire.

from *The New Yorker*

Like a Cat

◊   ◊   ◊

You want a dog
but you are like a cat,
though you hate cats,
which is a very catlike
position. I want a cat
but you're allergic
so we'll get a dog
who will be like me.
Besides, I realize that,
having you, I already
have a cat. You have
intense fixations, like
a cat. Though you're
tall and strong, you walk
lightly on the balls
of your feet, like a cat.
You're good at
everything you ever
try to do. In your
reticence you'd rather
not be written about or
analyzed, like a cat.
But you are very good
to look at, to study,
in your many moods
and attitudes, like a cat.
And your affection
is sudden and real,

radiating mystery
and heat beside me,
like a cat.

from *STAT®REC*

Metaphor-less

◇   ◇   ◇

The dryness dead center
Of deep pain. The bone on
Bone grinding that goes on
For months preceding
The surgery—that's the way
The parent whose child is using
Heroin again feels in the middle
Of the night unable to sleep, standing
At the bedroom window, looking out
Just barely conscious of what the moon
Looks like—drained, gray. The moon
Is a popular literary image—solipsistic
Misery, misplaced love. *Whatever.*
Tonight, it's nothing but a source
Of milky light, swinging high up in the sky
Shining weakly on the bleakness inside
And the bleakness outside that has
No other meaning but the cold
Un-crackable rock of itself.

from *Five Points*

Armed Neighbor

◇   ◇   ◇

I don't want to deny him the right to turn
His homestead into a fortress better prepared
For a siege than the Alamo. But I do wish
I could persuade him no columns of federal marshals
Are preparing to march from town to convert his property
Into a dark-site prison or a welfare hotel
For a mob of migrants too lazy
To make a homestead of their own.

I do wish I could persuade him he's lucky
That we live in an era where foot-thick walls
And narrow slits for windows have gone the way
Of the moat and drawbridge, an era when many neighbors,
Instead of hardening their perimeters,
Are blurring the boundaries between inside and outside
With elaborate decks and porches.

If safety is his concern, I'd like to convince him
He'd be better off investing in burglar alarms
And in cameras programmed to keep a record
Of all the cars that park near his property, so if
A couple of burglars wait till he leaves for work
To break in and steal his gun collection
He could give the police all the clues they needed
To solve the case in less than a day.

As for the pistol he's been taking to work for years
In a holster that isn't hidden, I don't accuse him
Of trying to mask with a symbol of power

A deep-seated feeling of insignificance.
I believe what he claims, that he hopes to save
Some fellow workers one day from a maniac
Running amok with a gun on the factory floor.

But I wish I could convince him it's just as likely
That one day a maniac will snatch at his gun
As he walks alone after work to his car,
That the gun will go off in the struggle
And the bullet, if it doesn't undo him, may undo a girl
Who happens that very moment to be playing hopscotch
Across the street in front of her tenement.

No doubt if I persuade him to leave his gun
At home, at least for a trial period,
On his usual foot patrol after supper
Around the neighborhood, he'll feel enfeebled,
Powerless to protect a neighbor from a menace
Should any creep near as night comes on.
But I'll assure him he may still be able
To offer assistance in emergencies.

Say he spots a glow in the sky
And follows it to a house in flames.
A gun would only get in the way
Of his dashing in to wake any sleepers
And carry a child out to a neighbor's lawn.

And if the parents carry the children
While he's left with a hamster cage or a fish bowl,
I'd like him to feel the task isn't beneath him.
Lending a hand, I'd tell him, is always dignified,
While being a hero is incidental.

from *New Letters*

TOI DERRICOTTE

An apology to the reader

◇　◇　◇

Let me first say that I regret sending the document out into the world. And I regret that (it having fallen into your hands) I am asking you to read it. However, having—by turns—abandoned and revised it for years, I decided it should be—even must be—given space.

I do this not as a performance of brutality to which I need your witness. I do it because it must exist as a reflection of its contrary. In my body the memories are lodged. The writing is a dim bulb on a black cord in the examiner's room.

I prefer you do not attempt to read it. I cannot help but feel responsible for your discomfort, so, as you read, you may feel me tugging at your fingers. The revelations are relentless, without a whisper of hope. (Without hope, what gives the poet permission?)

Completing a work of art necessitates a struggle to create balance and symmetry. I have been hampered by an idea of perfection. I have struggled to please one who mirrors back my unworthiness. But poetry is visceral; it re-creates the most primal sense of entitlement to breath and music, to life itself.

I have fixed together an internal form, like a tailor's bodice. I wear it as a self, stiff but useful, stitched together from scraps.

from *Prairie Schooner*

THOMAS DEVANEY

Brilliant Corners

◊   ◊   ◊

for Jennie C. Jones

The magic parts before they were burned-up and vacuumed.

A sound so light as if no one was there at all.

Your body a buffer between *the same word said at the same time* and other hyper jinx chances.

The dustup made the light look more grey than green.

Time was opened-up wider then, so wide in fact that even now it isn't all the way shut.

Horns, sirens, acoustic panels, plenty of *three people can keep a secret, if two are dead stories* to go around.

A late and great string quartet playing in the next room.

I couldn't tell where the music was coming from, and I didn't care.

I was back in high school practicing a clarinet concerto.

And for months, upended by the harp on the headphones in the Chopin waltz.

Walkman freewheeling Sony Walkman—

And only one other person in the world.

> It does not matter where we fell in, we did.

What she called AC/DC I called AC/DC. Though Monk wasn't Monk, he was MONK: avuncular, like an uncle with no glass in his glasses, poking his fingers *in* to show us.

Not silence, but the stillness of the world; and yet even being still didn't mean you couldn't scratch your nose.

How you once heard the sound of water running under a heavy manhole cover. The Great Spirit echoing in the old city pipes; the ghost river running under Allegheny Avenue.

Not sound, but the fact of sound.

Not sound or the fact of sound, but the fact of sound after the sound was gone.

from *The Brooklyn Rail*

Skin-Light

◇　◇　◇

My whole life I have obeyed it—

>   its every hunting. I move beneath it
>   as a jaguar moves, in the dark
>   liquid blading of shoulder.

The opened-gold field and glide of the hand,

>   light-fruited, and scythe-lit.

I have come to this god-made place—

>   Teotlachco, the ball court—
>   because the light called: *lightwards!*
>   and dwells here: Lamp-Land.

>   We touch the ball of light
>   to one another—split bodies desire-knocked
>   and stroked bright.
>   Light reshapes my lover's elbow,

>   a brass whistle.

I put my mouth there—mercy-luxed, and come, we both,

to light. It streams me.
A rush of scorpions—
      fast-light. A lash of breath—
         god-maker.

Light horizons her hip—springs an ocelot
cut of chalcedony and magnetite.
      Hip, limestone and cliffed,

slopes like light into her thigh—light-box, skin-bound.

Wind sways the calabash,
disrupts the light to ripple—light-struck,
      then scatter.

This is the war I was born toward, her skin,

its lake-glint. I desire—I thirst.
To be filled—light-well.

The light throbs everything, and songs

against her body, girdling the knee bone.
Our bodies—light-harnessed, light-thrashed.
      The bruising: bilirubin bloom,
         violet.

A work of all good yokes—blood-light—

to make us think the pain is ours
to keep, light-trapped, lanterned.
      That I asked for it. That I own it—
         lightmonger.

I am light now, or on the side of light—

light-head, light-trophied.
Light-wracked and light-gone.

Still, the sweet maize—an eruption
of light, or its feast,
        from the stalk
            of my lover's throat.

And I, light-eater, light-loving.

        from Poem-a-Day

Decline in the Adoration
of Jack-in-the-Pulpits

◊　◊　◊

The bijou Jack-in-the-Pulpit plant
looks like it's kneeling in dirt on dragon
knees in comparative darkness; conjures
a frocked man propagandizing at an altar;
if ingested raw its hooded bloom is poison—
Even so it's a part of paradise that won't survive behind glass.
What happens will go down in history as fable.
No one takes baths in the placid dark anymore.
There are too few hatmakers left.
Almost no silence to be found.
The days are sad and many people's backs hurt.
We are too occupied with our devices to notice
　　　　　what is crescendoing in the woods.
Cell phones are like bird coffins in our hands.
No one makes love without a mirror or a camera to witness—
often the sounds are recorded.
No one gets injured without posting pictures of the wound,
the veering drive to urgent care, the forlorn face of the nurse
sewing the stitches, the hot dog eaten afterward.
What is this ceaseless self-focus, but the hoopla,
　　　　　hue, and cry of an un-held baby?
A harelip never tended with a floral unguent.
No rain or sun on our skin, only the hum and haloes
of screens swaddling us. So when an angelic transvestite
in powder blue hot pants and lustrous butterfly wings
approaches us on the avenue with an offer of a piece of her soul,

along with a piece of *dulce de leche* ice-cream pie
and a shot of pink-tinted tequila, we are too vanished inside
a dull vortex, looking at facsimiles of flowers, fountains & females
to invite her inside and massage her exquisite feet.
Instead, we become frantic and apoplectic to find that we've lost
our chargers and it's 3:17 am and the Apple Store is closed
           and we don't notice the twenty-four-carat
                      cut-adrift angel
           walking away on black pavement
             swaying her veritable ass—
           ferrying her gifts out of reach.

           from *The Kenyon Review*

MARTÍN ESPADA

I Now Pronounce You Dead

◇ ◇ ◇

for Sacco and Vanzetti, executed August 23, 1927

On the night of his execution, Bartolomeo Vanzetti, immigrant
from Italia, fishmonger, anarchist, shook the hand of Warden Hendry
and thanked him for everything. *I wish to forgive some people for what
they are now doing to me,* said Vanzetti, blindfolded, strapped down
to the chair that would shoot two thousand volts through his body.

The warden's eyes were wet. The warden's mouth was dry. The warden
heard his own voice croak: *Under the law I now pronounce you dead.*
No one could hear him. With the same hand that shook the hand
of Bartolomeo Vanzetti, Warden Hendry of Charlestown Prison
waved at the executioner, who gripped the switch to yank it down.

The walls of Charlestown Prison are gone, to ruin, to dust, to mist.
Where the prison stood there is a school; in the hallways, tongues
speak the Spanish of the Dominican, the Portuguese of Cabo Verde,
the Creole of Haiti. No one can hear the last words of Vanzetti,
or the howl of thousands on Boston Common when they knew.

After midnight, at the hour of the execution, Warden Hendry
sits in the cafeteria, his hand shaking as if shocked, rice flying off
his fork, so he cannot eat no matter how the hunger feeds on him,
muttering the words that only he can hear: *I now pronounce you dead.*

from *Massachusetts Review*

41

The Analytic Hour

◊   ◊   ◊

1.

A suspension in time. A pause, a parenthesis,
   a rarefaction, an exstasis.
The error in the script: an inscrutable other.
   Not Erlebnis, but Erfahrung,

its frozen terror. The funhouse you feared
   with its jeering maze of mirrors
where all reference reveals the uncongealed
   humors of its clowning tutelar.

2.

To my right, the single window an oculus
   onto the world: a tiled roof,
each tile gently overlapping the one below,
   hiding the nails, joints, seams,

the structure that keeps the whole in place,
   armored against the elements.
Above the neat row of houses, the contrails
   of a jet, its trail cleaving the sky.

3.

What are you thinking? I could ask you
       the same, but to no avail.
I am thinking of the window. Refulgence.
       Luminosity. The grand fiat.

The diaphanous curtains hung between
       the light and me—I who see
but do not see. More light, for god's sake,
       more light. Let there be light.

4.

I free-associate, though nothing is free.
       Free, feral, ferrous. A rusty
outdoor faucet, the one that watered
       my mother's garden,

its brass now weathered to verdigris.
       The handle won't budge.
A drop of water hangs vestigial from
       the stiff rounded lip.

5.

Who needs a garden? Thy will be done.
       New spirits inhabit
the stations of hearth and home. Take them:
       I give them to you.

The clock avows the hour. Nothing happens.
       Nothing ever happens.
An exercise in detachment, divestiture.
       I learn how not to need.

from *The American Scholar*

Canzone in Blue, Then Bluer

◇　◇　◇

There wasn't music as much as there was
terror so the music became as much a
part of the terror as the terror it-
self with the swell of the arpeggio building and
breaking, building and breaking, upon the shores
of you. Your shores washed slowly away but
not slowly enough, you still feel it, every grain
of sand a note going under, bluing the
body, granular and wet. This has happened
before. You weren't special. You belonged to
no group of any more particular concern
than another. But the music has become
you. The hurt coming out, from your open mouth, could
open a grave. Let every done-wrong haint throw
its head back and groan. Not done-wrong as in some-
body loved left, somebody is always left,
but done-wrong as in someone who deserved to live
as much as anyone else died by another's hands
or neglect or the indifference of someone
who cared less or just not about you. And you sang
like you cried until the music of leaving,
of long-gone became you. Does it matter how
many strings? It only takes one to make this
music. But let's say it was the sound of
a choir that accompanied the run of
blood down a leg. Let's say a violin sped

its notes down the side of a neck, a tirade
of pricks. Or a high C from a voice thrown sharp
as the pieces of skull a bullet through the
head would leave. Or the river, the river rush-
ing cold and rock-bottomed, with its own furious
song carries you with it, sings you right over
the falls. That is when terror is not blue but bluer,
blue as capillaries bursting from an eye,
blue as the vein under this razor, blue as
the skin beat so far it breaks into song, a
song like this. And I've sung this so many times dear
my voice has almost given way, and I'm so scared.

from *Asheville Poetry Review*

Guantanamera

◊ ◊ ◊

Nothing lingers on the lips like a death song,
my mother says, while shredding cassava

and invoking the spirits—
            Celia Cruz   José Martí—

or singing blood verse, a church lady
working the line, refugee intake.

Celia rolling pride through a gap
in her teeth, a cry that is palm tree split

middle-of-night lightning,
and my mother, hands full of seashell witchcraft,

hands full of rooster feather prayer,
says the ocean tastes different

once we've drunk it all, once we've bongo beat
to water bumping on a home-baked raft: we

pilgrims who sway and dip to the sky because
how close to almost-death is our trombone shriek

and even if we deny it—our blackness
our *fufú plátano quimbombó*-ness,

we end up riding the rhythm
on the right pause, roaring lineage on our hips

and in our swings when
we are dancing across the oceans like gods.

from *Cincinnati Review*

Update

◇   ◇   ◇

My dresses huddle in their closet.
No histrionics, no tears. They're undaunted,
unhaunted, since you disappeared.
Torture by laundry and mothball
is all I can offer them, though it's Christmas.
And despite the holiday, there's endless
wrestling on TV. Is that your nudge to me:
toughen up and roll with the punches?
Here on earth, another rough era is birthed.
Sea monsters burst from the surf,
through waves of what we've mistaken
for civilization. Any advice from the heights
where you're exiled? Some flutter of succor
to dial back the angst to a dull roar? Though you
are no more, the onions you planted, shoved
underground, too, send shoots into this persistent
rain, feelers like little green racks of antlers. Your
bougainvillea's ablaze with reds, magentas
and noisy finches. The maple tree lost her leaves,
then grew six inches. I'll slip on my coat and hike
to the river, praying I see your image, fringed
by whitewater, in it. If I do, can you gift
me with savagery-management tips, or some
comforting sign, surreptitiously, via the mist?

from *Ploughshares*

Virgil, Hey

◇　◇　◇

Ah me! I find myself middle-aged divorced lost
In the forest dark of my failures mortgage & slack breasts
It's hard to admit nobody wants to do me anymore
Not even Virgil will lead me down to his basement rental

Take a look at my firstborn son
Who put me on three months' bedrest
For whom I bled on the emergency room floor
Who declaims his device sucks
Stabs holes in his bedroom wall
Complains his ATV's too slow
Who plots to run away to join terrorists
He'd rather die than do math

And the little one ripped
From my womb in the surgery room
I pierced my nipples to unblock her milk
Who pours lemonade on the floor for skating
Howls in rage cause her cake isn't pretty
Carved No Mom on her door with scissors
Who says, No fence but you're kinda fat
She'd rather die than wear underpants

Virgil, hey! Send me down
To the second circle of hell where I belong
With those whom Love separated from Reason
Where an infernal hurricane will blast me

Hither & thither with no hope ever no comfort
Rather than drive these two to school this morning
And suffer forever with the other mothers

from *The New Republic*

YONA HARVEY

Dark and Lovely
After Take-Off (A Future)

◊   ◊   ◊

Nobody straightens their hair anymore.
Space trips & limited air supplies will get you conscious quick.

My shea-buttered braids glow planetary
as I turn unconcerned, unburned by the pre-take-off bother.

"Leave it all behind," my mother'd told me,
sweeping the last specs of copper thread from her front porch steps &

just as quick, she turned her back to me. Why
had she disappeared so suddenly behind that earthly door?

"Our people have made progress, but, perhaps,"
she'd said once, "not enough to guarantee safe voyage

to the Great Beyond," beyond where Jesus
walked, rose, & ascended in the biblical tales that survived

above sprocket-punctured skylines &
desert-dusted runways jeweled with wrenches & sheet metal scraps.

She'd no doubt exhale with relief to know
ancient practice & belief died hard among the privileged, too.

Hundreds of missions passed & failed, but here
I was strapped in my seat, anticipating—what exactly?

Curved in prayer or remembrance of a hurt
so deep I couldn't speak. Had that been me slammed to the ground, cuffed,

bulleted with pain as I danced with pain
I couldn't shake loose, even as the cops aimed pistols at me,

my body & mind both disconnected
& connected & unable to freeze, though they shouted "freeze!"

like actors did on bad television.
They'd watched & thought they recognized me, generic or bland,

without my mother weeping like Mary,
Ruby, Idella, Geneava, or Ester stunned with a grief

our own countrymen refused to see, to
acknowledge or cease initiating, instigating, &

even mocking in the social networks,
ignorant frays bent and twisted like our DNA denied

but thriving and evident nonetheless—
You better believe the last things I saw when far off lifted

were *Africa Africa Africa*
Africa Africa Africa Africa Africa . . .

& though it pained me to say it sooner:
the unmistakable absence of the Great Barrier Reef.

from Poem-a-Day

Dancing

◇   ◇   ◇

The radio clicks on—it's poor swollen America,
Up already and busy selling the exhausting obligation
Of happiness while intermittently debating whether or not
A man who kills fifty people in five minutes
With an automatic weapon he has bought for the purpose
Is mentally ill. Or a terrorist. Or if terrorists
Are mentally ill. Because if killing large numbers of people
With sophisticated weapons is a sign of sickness—
You might want to begin with fire, our early ancestors
Drawn to the warmth of it—from lightning,
Must have been, the great booming flashes of it
From the sky, the tree shriveled and sizzling,
Must have been, an awful power, the odor
Of ozone a god's breath; or grass fires,
The wind whipping them, the animals stampeding,
Furious, driving hard on their haunches from the terror
Of it, so that to fashion some campfire of burning wood,
Old logs, must have felt like feeding on the crumbs
Of the god's power and they would tell the story
Of Prometheus the thief, and the eagle that feasted
On his liver, told it around a campfire, must have been,
And then—centuries, millennia—some tribe
Of meticulous gatherers, some medicine woman,
Or craftsman of metal discovered some sands that,
Tossed into the fire, burned blue or flared green,
So simple the children could do it, must have been,
Or some soft stone rubbed to a powder that tossed
Into the fire gave off a white phosphorescent glow.
The word for *chemistry* from a Greek—some say Arabic—

Stem associated with metal work. But it was in China
Two thousand years ago that fireworks were invented—
Fire and mineral in a confined space to produce power—
They knew already about the power of fire and water
And the power of steam: 100 BC, Julius Caesar's day.
In Alexandria, a Greek mathematician produced
A steam-powered turbine engine. Contain, explode.
"The earliest depiction of a gunpowder weapon
Is the illustration of a fire-lance on a mid-12th century
Silk banner from Dunhuang." Silk and the silk road.
First Arab guns in the early fourteenth century. The English
Used cannons and a siege gun at Calais in 1346.
Cerignola, 1503: the first battle won by the power of rifles
When Spanish "arquebusters" cut down Swiss pikemen
And French cavalry in a battle in southern Italy.
(Explosions of blood and smoke, lead balls tearing open
The flesh of horses and young men, peasants mostly,
Farm boys recruited to the armies of their feudal overlords.)
How did guns come to North America? 2014,
A headline: DIVERS DISCOVER THE *SANTA MARIA*
One of the ship's Lombard cannons may have been stolen
By salvage pirates off the Haitian reef where it had sunk.
And Cortés took Mexico with 600 men, 17 horses, 12 cannons.
And LaSalle, 1679, constructed a seven-cannon barque,
Le Griffon, and fired his cannons upon first entering the continent's
Interior. The sky darkened by the terror of the birds.
In the dream time, they are still rising, swarming,
Darkening the sky, the chorus of their cries sharpening
As the echo of that first astounding explosion shimmers
On the waters, the crew blinking at the wind of their wings.
Springfield Arsenal, 1777. Rock Island Arsenal, 1862.
The original Henry rifle: a sixteen shot .44 caliber rimfire
Lever-action, breech-loading rifle patented—it was an age
Of tinkerers—by one Benjamin Tyler Henry in 1860,
Just in time for the Civil War. Confederate casualties
In battle: about 95,000. Union casualties in battle:
About 110,000. Contain, explode. They were throwing
Sand into the fire, a blue flare, an incandescent green.
The Maxim machine gun, 1914, 400–600 small caliber rounds
Per minute. The deaths in combat, all sides, 1914–1918

Was 8,042,189. Someone was counting. Must have been.
They could send things whistling into the air by boiling water.
The children around the fire must have shrieked with delight
1920: Iraq, the peoples of that place were "restive,"
Under British rule and Winston Churchill
Invented the new policy of "aerial policing" which amounted,
Sources say, to bombing civilians and then pacifying them
With ground troops. Which led to the tactic of terrorizing civilian
Populations in World War II. Total casualties in that war,
Worldwide: soldiers, 21 million; civilians, 27 million.
They were throwing sand into the fire. The ancestor who stole
Lightning from the sky had his guts eaten by an eagle.
Spreadeagled on a rock, the great bird feasting.
They are wondering if he is a terrorist or mentally ill.
London, Dresden. Berlin. Hiroshima, Nagasaki.
The casualties difficult to estimate. Hiroshima:
66,000 dead, 70,000 injured. In a minute. Nagasaki:
39,000 dead; 25,000. There were more people killed,
100,000, in more terrifying fashion in the firebombing
Of Tokyo. Two arms races after the ashes settled.
The other industrial countries couldn't get there
Fast enough. Contain, burn. One scramble was
For the rocket that delivers the explosion that burns humans
By the tens of thousands and poisons the earth in the process.
They were wondering if the terrorist was crazy. If he was
A terrorist, maybe he was just unhappy. The other
Challenge afterwards was how to construct machine guns
A man or a boy could carry: lightweight, compact, easy to assemble.
First a Russian sergeant, a Kalashnikov, clever with guns
Built one on a German model. Now the heavy machine gun,
The weapon of European imperialism through which
A few men trained in gunnery could slaughter native armies
In Africa and India and the mountains of Afghanistan,
Became "a portable weapon a child can operate."
The equalizer. So the undergunned Vietnamese insurgents
Fought off the greatest army in the world, so the Afghans
Fought off the Soviet army using Kalashnikovs the CIA
Provided to them. They were throwing powders in the fire
And dancing. Children's armies in Africa toting AK-47s
That fire thirty rounds a minute. A round is a bullet.

An estimated 500 million firearms on the earth.
100 million of them are Kalashnikov-style semiautomatics.
They were dancing in Orlando, in a club. Spring night.
Gay Pride. The relation of the total casualties to the history
Of the weapon that sent exploded metal into their bodies—
30 rounds a minute, or 40, is a beautifully made instrument,
And in America you can buy it anywhere—and into the history
Of the shaming culture that produced the idea of Gay Pride—
They were mostly young men, they were dancing in a club,
A spring night. The radio clicks on. Green fire. Blue fire.
The immense flocks of terrified birds still rising
In wave after wave above the waters in the dream time.
Crying out sharply. As the French ship breasted the vast interior
Of the new land. America. A radio clicks on. The Arabs,
A commentator is saying, require a heavy hand. Dancing.

from *The American Poetry Review*

American Sonnet for My Past and Future Assassin

◇ ◇ ◇

For her last birthday I found in a used New Jersey
Toy store, a six inch Amiri Baraka action figure
With three different outfits: an elaborately colored
Dashiki with afro pick; a black linen Leninist getup,
And a sports coat with elbow patches & wool Kangol.
Accessories include an ink pen & his father's pistol.
If you dip him in bathwater, he will leak
The names of his abandoned children. Pull a string,
He sings "Preface to a Twenty Volume Suicide Note"
Sweeter than the sweetest alto to ever sing
In the Boys Choir of Harlem. The store clerk tried
Selling me the actual twenty volume note LeRoi Jones
Wrote the night before Baraka put a bullet in him.
I would've bought it. But I had no room in my suitcase.

from *Harvard Review*

Roll Under the Waves

◊   ◊   ◊

we roll under the waves
not above them we bodysurf and somehow we lose
the momentum there are memories trailing us empty orange
and hot pink bottles of medicines left behind
buried next to a saguaro there are baby backpacks
and a thousand shoes and a thousand gone steps
leading in the four directions each one without destinations
there are men lying facedown forever and women
dragging under the fences and children still running with
torn faces all the way to Tucson leathery and peeling
there are vigilantes with skull dust on their palms
and the trigger and the sputum and the moon with
its pocked hope and its blessings and its rotations into the spikes
there is a road forgotten with a tiny sweet roof of twigs
and a black griddle threaded with songs like the one
about el contrabando from El Paso there is nothing
a stolen land forgotten too a stolen life branded and
tied and thrown into the tin patrol box with flashes of trees
and knife-shaped rivers and the face of my mother Luz and
water running next to the animals still thrashing choking
their low burnt violin muffled screams in rings
of roses across the mountains

from *Love's Executive Order*

Stranger by Night

◇   ◇   ◇

After I lost
my peripheral vision
I started getting sideswiped
by pedestrians cutting
in front of me
almost randomly
like memories
I couldn't see coming
as I left the building
at twilight
or stepped gingerly
off the curb
or even just crossed
the wet pavement
to the stairs descending
precipitously
into the subway station
and I apologized
to every one
of those strangers
jostling me
in a world that had grown
stranger by night.

from *The Threepenny Review*

Ledger

◊ ◊ ◊

Tchaikovsky's *Eugene Onegin* is 3,592 measures.
A voice kept far from feeling is heard as measured.
What's wanted in desperate times are desperate measures.
Pushkin's unfinished *Onegin*: 5,446 lines.

No visible tears measure the pilot's grief
as she Lidars the height of an island: five feet.
Fifty, its highest leaf.
She logs the years, the weathers, the tree has left.

A million fired-clay bones—animal, human—
set down in a field as protest
measure 400 yards long, 60 yards wide, weigh 112 tons.
The length and weight and silence of the bereft.

Bees do not question the sweetness of what sways beneath them.
One measure of distance is meters. Another is *li*.
Ten thousand li can be translated: "far."
For the exiled, *home* can be translated "then," translated "scar."

One liter
of Polish vodka holds twelve pounds of potatoes.
What we care about most, we call *beyond measure*.
What matters most, we say *counts*. Height now is treasure.

On this scale of one to ten, where is eleven?
Ask all you wish, no twenty-fifth hour will be given.

Measuring mounts—like some Western bar's mounted elk head—
our catalogued vanishing unfinished heaven.

from *Times Literary Supplement*

Sunflowers

◇   ◇   ◇

Standing in front of Van Gogh's portrait,
the winter one with the bandage and heavy
green overcoat, blue hat with black fur,
every stroke pained as the mangled face
he is showing us, mangled but repairing
as if he's lived through something worth
pleading, shellacked and deft on canvas—
my son asks *What happened to his head?*
He's still a kid and doesn't know the story,
the unbearability of loving the ones who leave.
When I don't answer he eats the quiet,
the way when I turn down the radio's litany
of casualties, he hunkers like a monk
burying his head in a bowl of Cheerios.
But really, what is there to say about that—
A photo of my brother patrolling a field
of sunflowers in Afghanistan. It'll be years
before he understands the ear, that presence
implicates the missing. It'll be just after
school lets out, driving to the grocery store,
and he will tell me about another Van Gogh,
a vase of sunflowers, they studied in art class.
Simple task: To record in journals how each
differs, this head from that, this paint from that.
We will be crossing the creek bridge
and he will be mid-sentence and I will be
thinking summer—Roadsides lined with flowers
in black buckets, and birds taking seed
out of ones we plant along the garden fence,

wondering if he knows about Gauguin,
the Yellow House in Arles. And just when
I feel I am almost useful, he will ask:
Did your brother have to kill anyone?
What I don't know becomes signature.
What I can't say becomes silence
and silence scores the mind, and the mind,
never letting go, takes the marks and makes
a house of the cuttings. But all that's outside
the frame. We are here now, looking
backward and forward at a painting of a man
injured by love. And if I had the means,
I'd ditch the day, turn all elsewheres noise,
and hold truant the coma calm of a museum.
And if I had the heart not to feel this forever
is not the one my son wants, I'd break it,
strew it against the bric-a-brac and static.
To stay still this long is a terrible thing to ask.

from *The American Poetry Review*

All Praise Cecil Taylor

◇ ◇ ◇

> Rhythm is the Life of Space of Time danced through.
> —Cecil Taylor

Them laugh them cry them fingers flip wise
Troll the riverbed dead not dead not dead
Once after the concert you told me it was not after the concert
This is the concert is just what you said
I remember that now along with dead not dead not dead
So a blew note blows trill still the hurricane of silence
You mentioned how the string got unstrung and when it rung
That's where it begun so begin again a little closer to the end
Where the bend won't bend and the bang hangs a blend
Right at the point and left with the joint just hammer
Hammer the pale night nail (hammer the pale night nail)
The jawdropper corral where the pedal dance flail
That's the cozy up to it reborn, where the Stop sign is a square
Baby understands, rocks the baby grand and rolls the key
Till the lock screams "I Give" and all the dough
Comes rolling up to Heaven's creak, squeak squeak

from *Black Renaissance Noire*

The Bathers, Cassis

◇ ◇ ◇

It's too hot to think much about the ochre cliffs of Cap Canaille
or the moan of a tour boat's engines grinding through the aquamarine
                                        of the Mediterranean.
I'm inside measuring the width of the white ribbon of the wake
like a long skin shedding itself from the exoskeleton of a Zodiac boat,
assessing valuations of finitude amongst my household property,
gazing at the bathers as they take turns diving off the limestone promontory
                                        below and to my left,
lazily frog-kicking through the cerulean waters of Port-de-Cassis.

Their bodies are pale as salamanders as they scoot through
                                        the zaffre and viridian
back to the rock-toothed shore where they pull themselves up,
amphibian-like, stunning the air with their glistening bodies.
It is a sensate joy that releases like ecstatic vapor
from off their skins and sea-drenched hair.
A hand has touched them and *pass'd over their bodies*,
                                        but not over mine.

If I were to walk a serrated shore, worn by wind and the idylls
                                        of companionship,
I'd be twenty again and arrogant as Icarus
                                making survey of his father's domain,
scanning the surface of the sea for a boil of sardines
                                        glinting like a scatter of coins.
Preposterously, I'd glance neither to my left or to my right,
and launch myself straight into a dive of my own,
unshowy and silent as I cut the immaculate waters,
joyous only in the theater of my own being, alone

as the brown salts that dry on the stoic, limestone lips of the sea,
unconsecrated by touch, the liquidinous mask of my face
submerged and upturned, trailing shrouds of sapphire and indigo.

from *The Kenyon Review*

Sympathy of a Clear Day

◇   ◇   ◇

By melon carts and feral cats skinning off adobe
walls, we thread the white heat of day on the square,
to the café minarets level at our eyes, vapor coils
of virgin snow peaks through them, ready to spring.

Travel is sympathy. Not so, you point at what's below:
birds and monkeys shuck to perform by their cages;
snakes rise in fragrant droppings on carpets children
squat with whisks while tourist dollars and coins fill baskets.

Souks edge the lubric traffic. Commerce, from the good
cool of this café, prowls and gnaws the city to the bone.
Mighty caravans appear still with oaths and murmurs
from across the equator, no longer with tents, for cheap

hotels proliferate as madly as the war raged for oil.
From this height we are in a spell of fabrics, lavender
and saffron, those loggias of black soften in the haze
glow basalt and move in fluid swaths against shadows.

Bless Churchill's cruel, romantic eyes, in one regard,
for painting the sky's fragile lilac and radio wafer,
no longer audible, over the bazaar's broken watercolours.
His self-centered ego now turns unseen, incessant drones.

"To celebrate," you tell me with mock triumph, "a holiday
is to become free for the unaccustomed day: the clear day."
The clear day I repeat, then shudder remembering another
phrase, the God-land compressed within itself, and remind you.

Any reprieve but none from the unredeemable world.
Weighted voices. Clouds cover the propane tank on the terrace;
we come down to go to the desert, that final archive where
dragnet of stars blanch at sunset over travelers in slow progress.

from *Freeman's*

DIDI JACKSON

The Burning Bush

◇ ◇ ◇

for Brianne Ortt (1979–2016)

An entire alphabet can be stuttered in a few gunshots.
So often it's the boyfriend spiraling down the chamber:
his words lodged in the barrel behind the bullet fast and frenzied.

We all wonder why the trash at the dump
never stops burning, why the blind look to the wind.
The rain stumbles outside the window:
the *tombé* before the heavy *pas de bourrée* of storm.

Basilica di San Marco in Venice speaks
two languages: Greek and Latin, and I am jealous
of those with two tongues like the white pine
whose trunk cracks and whose needles whistle
to the bilingual nuthatch.

The sun torches the tips of the trees
on a descent from a world where no woman is safe.
Even the man who loved her wanted her dead.

The burning bush is an invasive species,
yet cardinals and chickadees flock to its red seeds
and flamed leaves in the fall. I should cut it to a stump
and rot its roots, but instead I admire its show of color,
watching the damage as it spreads.

from *New England Review*

In Memory of Derek Alton Walcott

◊   ◊   ◊

1

Island traffic slows to a halt
as screeching gulls reluctant
to lift heavenward
congregate like mourners in salt-
crusted kelp, as the repellent
news spreads to colder shores:

Sir Derek is no more.
Bandwidths, clogged by streaming
tributes, carry the pitch
of his voice, less so his lines, moored
as they are to a fisherman's who strains
in the Atlantic

then hearing, too, drops his rod, the reel
unspooling like memory till
his gaped mouth matches
the same look in his wicker creel,
that frozen shock, eyes marble
a different catch.

Pomme-Arac trees, sea grapes,
and laurels sway, wrecked having lost
one who heard their leaves'

rustic dialect as law, grasped
their bows as edicts from the first
garden that sowed faith—

and believe he did, astonished
at the bounty of light, like Adam,
over Castries, Cas-
en-Bas, Port of Spain, the solace
of drifting clouds, rains like hymns
then edens of grass,

ornate winds on high verandas
carrying spirits who survived
that vile sea crossing,
who floated up in his stanzas,
the same souls Achille saw alive,
the ocean their coffin—

faith, too, in sunsets, horizons
whose auric silhouettes divide
and spawn reflection,
which was his pen's work, devotion
twinned with delight, divining
like a church sexton.

Poetry is empty without
discipline, without piety,
he cautions somewhere,
even his lesser rhymes amount
to more than wrought praise but amplify
his poems as high prayer.

So as to earn their wings above,
pelicans move into tactical
formation then fly
low like jet fighters in honor of
him, nature's mouth, their aerial
salute and goodbye.

2

Derek, each journey we make,
whether Homeric or not,
follows the literal wake
of some other craft's launch,

meaning to sense the slightest
motions in unmoving waters
is half the apprentice's
training before he oars

out, careful to coast, break-
ing English's calm surface.
What you admired in Eakins
in conversation at some café

(New Orleans? Philly?) was
how his rower seemed to listen
to ripples on the Schuylkill as
much as to his breath, both silent

on his speaking canvas.
Gratitude made you intolerant
of the rudeness of the avant-
garde or any pronouncements

of the "new," for breathing is
legacy and one's rhythm,
though the blood's authentic
transcription, hems us

to ancestors like a pulse. This,
I fathom, is what you meant
when exalting the merits
of a fellow poet: *that man*

is at the center of language,
at the center of the song.

Yet a reader belongs to another age
and, likely to list our wrongs

more than the strict triumphs
of our verse, often retreats
like a vanished surf, spume
frothing on a barren beach.

The allure of an artist's works
these days is measured
by his ethics, thus our books,
scrubbed clean, rarely mention

the shadowless dark that settles
like an empire over a page. Your nib,
like the eye of a moon, flashed into sight
the source of Adam's barbaric cry.

3

Departed from paradise,
each *Nobody* a sacrifice,
debating whose lives matter
whereon a golden platter

our eyes roll dilated by hate
from Ferguson to Kuwait.
You, *maître*, gave in laughter
but also for the hereafter

an almost unbearable
truth: we are the terrible
history of warring births
destined for darkest earth.

So as cables of optic lights
bounce under oceans our white
pain, codified as they are
and fiber-layered in Kevlar,

we hear ourselves in you,
where "race" exiles us to
stand lost as single nations
awaiting your revelations.

A shirtless boy, brown as bark,
gallops alongshore, bareback
and free on a horse until he fades,
a shimmering, all that remains.

from *The Paris Review* and *Poetry Daily*

from "Last Will and Testament"

◊　◊　◊

1.

Because cemeteries are too pricy
I would like to be deposited on a public bench
and not in the earth
but in the middle of September
at the end of wonder:
wrap me in newspapers, darlings,
and run!

I want to live my death
on a public bench
next to a barbershop—
die, when it is time to cut my hair so I can save four dollars!
I was always happy in barbershops.
Now happiness,
come blow your nose in my hands—

I want to die on a public bench—
those who watch me in
the street
say
something in him wants to be entered and picked clean.

Be careless, life!
Wrap me in newspaper on a park bench
so some enterprising schoolchild

can filch from my eyes
two dimes
and replace them with two US postal stamps.

3.

From a park bench I watch my pregnant wife chase pigeons on the piazza

Katie!
You have got nerve!

In my final 17 hours:
I have so much love, too much love, I cannot control myself!

Plan A:
I shoot myself. And the earth is mine.

but the earth has never been mine!
Those who say the planet is theirs should pay higher taxes!

*

Katie and I are kissing at 3 oclock and at 4 oclock and at 5 oclock

our kisses interrupted only
by the ritual blowing of my nose

*

Plan B:
—I want a pillow-fight
with a woman lit by freckles! I want to live in a large apartment of her mouth.

A serious girl
who when in the middle of the night I wake her with kisses

laughs.
You must control yourself, sir.

Professor, you must control yourself!

8.

I, a person exhausted by his own happiness—
                                    I have so much love this morning, I
cannot control myself

In these last eight minutes

from a park bench
I want to step again and again on cement of life

I, in this my 41st year of trespass on earth,
watch death:

in a body
that stands on a platform

watches death, like a lone cross-country train, transport a spark.

9.

Snow has eaten $\frac{1}{4}$ of me

yet I believe
against all evidence

these snowflakes
are my letters of recommendation

here is a man worth falling on.

from *The Paris Review*

We May No Longer Consider the End

◇   ◇   ◇

The time of birds died sometime between
When Robert Kennedy, Jr., disappeared and the Berlin
Wall came down. Hope was pro forma then.
We'd begun to talk about shelf-life. Parents
Thought they'd gotten somewhere. I can't tell you
What to make of this now without also saying that when
I was 19 and read in a poem that *the pure products of America go crazy*
I felt betrayed. My father told me not to whistle because I
Was a girl. He gave me my first knife and said to keep it in my right
Hand and to keep my right hand in my right pocket when I walked at night.
He showed me the proper kind of fist and the sweet spot on the jaw
To leverage my shorter height and upper-cut someone down.
There were probably birds on the long walk home but I don't
Remember them because pastoral is not meant for someone
With a fist in each pocket waiting for a reason.

from Poem-a-Day

Soft Targets

◊   ◊   ◊

It was good getting drunk in the undulant city.
Whiskey lopping off the day's fear.

Dawn came with an element of Xanax.
Dusk came and I dumbed myself down.

Where there were brides, grooms—
these bored boysoldiers with iPhones and guns.

I'm a soft target, you're a soft target,
and the city has a hundred hundred thousand softs.

The pervious skin, the softness of the face,
the wrist inners, the hips, the lips, the tongue,

the global body,
its infinite permutable softnesses.

★

Soft targets, soft readers, drinkers,
pedestrians in rain—

In the failing light we walked out
and now we share a room with it

(would you like to read to me in the soft,
would you like to enter me in the soft,

would you like a lunch of me in the soft,
in its long delirium?).

The good news is we have each other.
The bad news is: Kalashnikov assault rifles,

submachine guns, pistols, ammunition,
four boxes packed with thousands of small steel balls.

★

O you who want to slaughter us,
we'll be dead soon enough what's the rush.

And this our only world.
As you can see it has a problem.

As you can see the citizens are hanging heavy.
The citizens' minds are out.

Eros, Eros, in Paris we stayed all night
in a seraphic cocktail haze

despite the blacked-out theater,
the shuttered panes.

Tonight we're the most tender of soft targets,
pulpy with alcohol and all a-sloth.

Monsieur can we get a few more?
There are unmistakable signs of trouble,

but we have days and days still.
Let's be giddy, maybe. Time lights a little fire.

We are animal hungry down to our intricate bones.
O beautiful habits of living, let me dwell on you awhile.

from *The American Poetry Review*

Higher Calling

◇ ◇ ◇

how you, heathen passenger, gonna help the nun
sitting across the aisle on a LA bound flight
dressed in drab habit, bone scapular & bright belief
ovahstand she needs to get off the damn cell phone?
her tongue central american cataclysm & barrio Jah.
who am i to tell a mercy angel the rule she must close

her flip phone? my sisters held sister bertrille close
in the early seventies. sally field as flying nun
could do no wrong. when she took to sky, Almighty Jah
lifting palms to bring her near, frock as kite, flight
rebuking surf board. the vestal in 13D cups phone
with large hands, hands large enough for holy, belief

like my auntie, mama's third sister, who shares belief
and the flying nun's last name. pastor bonnell is closer
to the Prophet. her whisper fragile on the telephone
when we talk of mama. both labored for stiff anglican nuns
over thirty years at the hospital their nine children took flight
in a small town uncertain if black people could know Jah.

uncles, cousins and friends offer daily petitions to Jah
to climb inside aunties breaths, feed her good news and belief.
she is the last matriarch and we are selfish. please don't fly
from us, we pray. we want to shelter her, wrap her close
in cotton and light. weekday mornings they come, the nuns
who wash her body, chanting glory. on weekends they phone

hallelujahs. if i ask, will this saint three feet away send phone
mercies to my auntie? will frail pastor bonnell decipher Jah
in spanish? she's sending texts at 45,000 feet now, this rogue nun
who exorcises airplane procedure. the flight attendant believes
otherwise. his syrupy sweet requests fall mute as he bends close
yet again. his tongue is not sanctified. this anointed saint flies

heavenward hourly. only twice daily for the exasperated flight
attendant. who is the service provider for sister's cell phone
hotline to Jesus? five hours on southwest, embrace of sun close
and blinding. city of the angels not far. before every take-off i ask Jah
for traveling mercies, beg for a protective hedge in queasy belief
give thanks for safe journey. extra blessings to sit next to a nun.

from *Gulf Coast*

The Undressing

◇ ◇ ◇

Listen,
she says.

I'm listening, I answer
and kiss her chin.

Obviously, you're not, she says.
I kiss her nose and both of her eyes.
I can do more than one thing at a time,
I tell her. Trust me.
I kiss her cheeks.

You've heard of planting lotuses in a fire, she says.
You've heard of sifting gold from sand.

You know
perfumed flesh, in anklets, and spirit, unadorned,
take turns at lead and follow,
one in action and repose.

I kiss her neck and behind her ear.

But there are things you need reminded of, she says.
So remind me, Love, I say.

There are stories we tell ourselves, she says.
There are stories we tell others.
Then there's the sum
of our hours
death will render legible.

I unfasten the top button of her blouse
and nibble her throat with more kisses.
Go on, I say, I'm listening.
You better be, she says,
You'll be tested.

I undo her second,
her third, fourth, and last buttons quickly,
and then lean in
to kiss her collarbone.

She says, The world
is a story that keeps beginning.
In it, you have lived severally disguised:
bright ash, dark ash, mirror, moon;
a child waking in the night to hear the thunder;
a traveler stopping to ask the way home.
And there's still
the butterfly's night sea-journey to consider.

She says,
There are dreams we dream alone.
There are dreams we dream with others.
Then there's the lilac's secret
life of fire, of God
accomplished in the realm
of change and desire.

Pushing my hand away from her breast,
she keeps talking.

Alone, you dream in several colors: Blue,
wishing, and following the river.

In company, you dream in several others:
The time you don't have.
The time left over.
And the time it takes.

Your lamp has a triple wick:
remembering, questioning, and sheltering
made of your heart's and mind's agreement.
With it, you navigate the two seas: Day
with everything inside it;
night and all that's missing.

Meanwhile, I encounter difficulty
with her skirt knot, her fingers
confounding my progress,
as she goes on reviewing the doubtful points.

There are words we say in the dark.
There are words we speak in the light.
And sometimes they're the same words.

From where I've been sitting beside her,
I drop to one knee before her.

There's the word we give
to another.
There's the word we keep
with ourselves.
And sometimes they're the same word.

I slip one hand inside her blouse
and find her naked waist.
My other hand cradles her bare foot
from which her sandal has fallen.

A word has many lives.
Quarry, the word is game, unpronounceable.
Pursuant, the word is judge, pronouncing sentence.
Affliction, the word is a thorn, chastising.

I nudge her blouse open with my nose
and kiss her breastbone.

The initiating word
embarks, fixed between sighted wings, and

said, says, saying, none are the bird,
each just moments of the flying.

Doubling back, the word is infinite.
We circle ourselves,
the fruit rots in time,
and we're just passengers of our voices,
a bird in one ear crying, *Two!*
There are two worlds!
A bird in the other ear urging, *Through!*
Be through with this world and that world!

Her blouse lapses around her shoulders,
and I bend lower
to kiss her navel.

There are voices that wake us in the morning, she says.
There are voices that keep us up all night.

I lift my face and look into her eyes. I tell her,
The voices I follow
to my heart's shut house say,
A member of the late
and wounded light enjoined to praise,
each attends a song that keeps leaving.

Now, I'm fondling her breasts
and kissing them. Now,
I'm biting her nipples.
Not meaning to hurt her,
I'm hurting her a little,
and for these infractions I receive
the gentlest tugs at my ear.

She says,
All night, the lovers ask, *Do you love me?*
Over and over, the manifold beloved answers,
I love you. Back and forth,
merging, parting, folding, spending,
the lovers' voices

and the voices of the beloved
are the ocean's legion scaling earth's black bell,
their bright crested foam
the rudimentary beginnings
of bridges and wings, the dream of flying,
and the yearning to cross over.

Now, I'm licking her armpit. I'm inhaling
its bitter herbal fumes and savoring
its flavor of woodsmoke. I've undone
the knot to her skirt.

Bodies have circled bodies
from the beginning, she says,

but the voices of lovers
are Creation's most recent flowers, mere buds
of fire nodding on their stalks.

In love, we see
God burns hidden, turning
inside everything that turns.
And everything turns. Everything
is burning.

But all burning is not the same.
Some fires kindle freedom.
Some fires consolidate your bondage.
Do you know the difference?

I tell her, I want you to cup your breasts
in both of your hands
and offer them to me.
I want you to make them wholly
available to me.

I want to be granted open liberty
to leave many tiny
petal-shaped bruises,
like little kisses, all over you.

One and one is one, she says,
Bare shineth in bare.

Think, she says, of the seabirds
we watched at dawn
wheeling between that double blue
above and below them.

Defined by the gravity they defy,
they're the radiant shadows of what they resist,

and their turns and arcs in air
that will never remember them
are smiles on the face of the upper abyss.

Their flying makes
our inner spaciousness visible,
even habitable, restoring us
to infinity, we beings of non-being,
each so recent a creature,
and only lately spirits
learning how to love.

Shrill, their winged hungers
fill the attic blue
and signal our nagging jeopardy:
Death's bias, the slope
of our lives' every minute.

I want to hear you utter
the sharpest little cries of tortured bliss, I say,
like a slapped whelp spurt
exquisite gasps of delighted pleasure.

But true lovers know, she says,
hunger vacant of love is a confusion,
spoiling and squandering
such fruit love's presence wins.

The harvest proves the vine
and the hearts of the ones who tend it.

Everything else is gossip, guessing
at love's taste.

The menace of the abyss will be subdued, I say,
when I extort from you the most lovely cries
and quivering whispered pleas
and confused appeals of, *Stop*, and, *More*, and, *Harder.*

To love, she says. For nothing.
What birds, at home in their sky,
have dared more?
What circus performer,
the tent above him, the net below,
has risked so much? What thinker, what singer,
both trading for immortality?

Nothing saves him who's never loved.
No world is safe in that one's keeping.

We are travelers among other travelers
in an outpost by the sea.
We meet in transit, strange to each other,
like birds of passage between a country and a country,
and suffering from the same affliction of sleeplessness,
we find each other in the night

while others sleep. And between
the languages you speak and the several I remember,
we convene at the one we have in common,
a language neither of us were born to.
And we talk. We talk with our voices,
and we talk with our bodies.
And behind what we say,
the ocean's dark shoulders rise and fall all night,
the planet's massive wings ebbing and surging.

I tell her, Our voices shelter each other,
figures in a dream of refuge
and sanctuary.

Therefore, she says,
designations of North, South, East, and West,
Winter, Spring, Summer, Fall,
first son, second son, first daughter, second daughter,
change, but should correspond
to a current picture of the sky.

Each of our days fulfills
the measures of the sanctum
and its great tables' rounds.
The tables are not round.
Or, not only round.
At every corner,
opposites emerge, and you meet yourself.

I bow my head
and raise her foot to my mouth.

The pillared tables make a tower and a ladder.
They constitute the throne and the crown.
The crown is not for your
head. The throne is not your seat.
The days on which the tables stand
will be weighed and named.
And the days are not days.
Not the way you might understand days.
The tables summon the feast
and are an aspect of the host.

The smell of her foot
makes me think of saddles.
I lick her instep. I kiss her toes. I kiss her ankle.

Don't you kiss my lips
with that mouth, she says.

Gold bit, I think.
Tender spur, I think.

I kiss her calves. I kiss her knees.
I kiss the insides of her thighs.
I'm thinking about her hip bones. I'm tonguing
the crease where her thigh and her belly meet.

The rounds enclose the dance,
she says.

The round and the square together
determine the dimensions of the ark, she says.
The water is rising as we speak.

Are you paying attention? she says,
One and one is two.
You and me are three. A long arithmetic
no temporal hand reckons
rules galaxies and ants, exact
and exacting. Lovers obey,
sometimes contradicting human account.

The smell of her body
mixes with her perfume and makes me woozy.

All being tends toward fire, I say.

All being tends toward fire,
sayeth the fire, she says, correcting me.

All being tends toward water, sayeth the water,
Light, sayeth the light.
Wings, sayeth the birds.
Voice, sayeth the voiceless.

Give up guessing, she says, give up
these frightened gestures of a stooped heart.
You've done all your learning with others in mind.
You've done all your teaching thinking only of yourself.

Saving the world, you oppress people.
Abandon educated words and honored acts.
I want you to touch me
as if you want to know me, not arouse me.
And by God, sing! For nothing. Singing
is origin. Out of that modulated trembling, cosmic
and rooted in the primordial, quantum and concealed
in the temporal, all forms come to be.
Each thing, born of the myriad in concert, is one song
variously sung. Each thing flourishes by singing
and returns to vanish into song.

Your body is that whereby song is conducted.
Singing is that whereby your body is completed.
Singing develops all things.
Dying is singing's consummation.
Thinking, you remain entangled
in the coils of your world.
Singing, you marry all possible worlds.

You know, from all of your green and branching hours
that so soon die unremarked, general and redundant,
the hours you sing return to you in true scale and degree.
The hours you measure by singing return winged
and noted, throated, eyed, and whirring-hearted.
Return red-crested, blue-feathered, black-frocked,
striped, spotted, flecked, and fine-boned.
But don't stop there. Sing the tree,
sing the All, sing the lot
of your time, and uncover the body of the Word,
the compass of compasses. Sing change
and the principle of wings, the laws of seeing and hearing,
rising and falling, harmony and strife. Sing all
the ungraspable, the descending, ascending signatures,
and you sing the name of life.
Call every one of you to the feast.

Now, I'm drooling along her ribs.
I'm smacking my lips and tongue to better taste
her mossy, nutty, buttery, acrid sweat.

I know you more than I know, she says.
My body, astonished, answers to your body
without me telling it to.

Inside her is the safest place to be.
Inside her, with all those other mysteries,
those looming immensities:
god, time, death, childhood.

Listen, she says,
There's one more thing.
Regarding the fires, there are two.
Left and right, they grow wiser in the same house.
Up and down, the higher encases the lower,
and the lower clings to the higher.
Inner and outer, these two illuminations
are a thousand illuminations.

But I'm thinking,
My hands know things my eyes can't see.
My eyes see things my hands can't hold.

Listen, she says,
Never let the fires go out.
The paler, the hotter.

But I'm thinking, Pale alcove.
I'm thinking, My heart ripens with news
the rest of me waits to hear.

Are you listening?
But I'm not listening.
I'm thinking,

A nest of eggs for my crown, please.
And for my cushion, my weight in grapes.

I'm thinking, In one light,
love might look like siege.

In another light, rescue
might look like danger.

She says, The seeds of fire are ours to mother.
The dust, the shavings,
and all spare materials
must be burned in both fires,
the visible and the invisible.
Even the nails burned in them.
Even the tools burned.
And then the oven dismantled and burned.
Have you been hearing me?

For 20,000 years, human groups have thrived
by subtle and not so subtle mechanisms
of expulsion, exclusion, rejection, elimination, and murder.
Fractious multitudes made single
by false transcendences of state
and race. Unruly, disputatious, opining smithereens
and fractions come together over a sacrificial corpse,
a field of corpses, the earth covered with sacrifices.
Rivalrous fragments banded by irresistible want.
Legion united by unbounded appetite and fear
spawning new gods and false prophets every day.

Repugnant little pleasure machines,
mesmerized minions of the marketplace, sold
desire, sold conflict by greedy advertisers,
leaving love waxed cold in your wake,
famine, pestilence, and earthquakes your wake,
abomination, desolation, and tribulation your wake.
Violence your wake. One nation under the weapon.
One human city under the banner of murder.
One kalpa under the stumbling block.
One world under the sign of the scapegoat.
One species under the flag of the goat's head.
Well, it's too late for flags.
It's too late
for presidents. It's too late

for movie stars and the profit economy.
It's too late for plutonomy and precariate.
The war is on.
If love doesn't prevail,
who wants to live in this world?
Are you listening?

You thought my body was a tree
in which lived a bird. But now, can't you see
flocks alive in this blazing foliage?
Blue throngs, gold multitudes, and pale congregations.
And each member flits from branch to living branch.
Each is singing at different amplitudes and frequencies.
Each is speaking secrets that will ripen into sentence.
And their voices fan my fragrant smoldering.
Disclosing the indestructible body of law.
Ratifying ancient covenants. Establishing new cities.
And their notes time the budding
of your own flowering.
Die now. And climb up into this burning.

from *The American Poetry Review*

It Could Happen to You

◇ ◇ ◇

It's June 15, 2017, a Thursday,
fortieth anniversary of the infamous day
the Mets traded Tom Seaver to Cincinnati
and they're still losing

I mean we are

7 to 1 to the Washington Nationals
a team that didn't exist in 1977
the summer of a little tour in France
with Henry James
in a yellow Renault douze

the light a lovely gray
the rain a violin
concerto (Prokofiev's No. 2 in D Major)
and I had books to read

Huxley Woolf Forster and their enemy F. R. Leavis
Empson a little dull for my taste
also Freud on errors, Norman Mailer on orgasms,
James Baldwin in Paris
Dostoyevsky's *Notes from Underground* Part 1

and John Ashbery tells me he is reading *The Possessed*
translated as *The Demons* in the newfangled translation
while Ron and I stay faithful to Constance Garnett

I went upstairs stood on the terrace ate some cherries
admired the outline of trees in the dark

and Rosemary Clooney
sang "It Could Happen to You"

and I was a healthy human being, not a sick man
for the first summer in three years.

from *The New Yorker*

Cannibal Woman

◇ ◇ ◇

I'm looking for the right words, but all I can think of is:
        parachute or ice water.

There's nothing but this sailboat inside me, slowly trying
to catch a wind, maybe there's an old man on it, maybe a small child,

all I know is they'd like to go somewhere. They'd like to see the sail

straighten, go tense, and take them someplace. But instead they wait,
a little tender wave comes and leaves them
        right where they were all along.

How did this happen? No wind I can conjure anymore.

My father told me the story of a woman larger than a mountain,
who crushed redwoods with her feet, who could swim a whole lake

in two strokes—she ate human flesh and terrorized the people.

I loved that story. She was bigger than any monster, or Bigfoot,
        or Loch Ness creature—

a woman who was like weather, as enormous as a storm.

He'd tell me how she walked through the woods, each tree coming down,
branch to sawdust, leaf to skeleton, each mountain
        pulverized to dust.

Then they set a trap. A hole so deep she could not climb out of it.

(I have known that trap.)

Then people set her on fire with torches. So she could not eat them
anymore, could not steal their children or ruin their trees.

I liked this part too. The fire. I imagined how it burned her mouth,
her skin, and how she tried to stand but couldn't, how it almost felt
good to her—as if something was finally meeting her desire with desire.

The part I didn't like was the end, how each ash that flew up in the night
        became a mosquito, how she is still all around us
in the dark, multiplied.

I've worried my whole life that my father told me this because she is my
anger: first comes this hunger, then abyss, then fire,

and then a nearly invisible fly made of ash goes on and on eating mouthful
after mouthful of those I love.

from *SWWIM*

A Brief History
of the Future Apocalypse

◊   ◊   ◊

Worlds just keep on ending and
ending, ask anybody who survived

an earthquake in an ancient city
its people can't afford to bolt

to the bedrock, or lived to testify
about the tyrant who used his city's roofs

like planks to walk people off,
his country's rivers like alligator pits

he could lever open and drop a whole
angry nation into. Ask anyone

who has watched their own ribs emerge
as hunger pulls them out like a tide,

who watched bloody-sheet-wrapped
bodies from the epidemic burn,

or fled any of the wars to come.
The year I was eleven, I felt

the ground go airplane turbulent
beneath me. Its curt shuddering

brought down a bridge and a highway
I'd been under just the day before.

And I was not afraid, but should have been
the first time love fell in me like snow.

How could I know it would inter us
both, so much volcanic ash—

how could I not? The world must
end and I think it will keep ending

so long as we keep failing to heed
the simple prophesies of fact—

hot-mouthed coal-breathing machines
fog our crystal ball, war is a trapdoor

sprung open in the earth that a whole
generation falls through, love ends,

if no one errs, in death. When
my love died, I remember thinking

this happens to people every day,
just—today, it's our world

crashing like an unmanned plane
into the jungle of all I've ever

had to feel, or imagine knowing.
It feels terrible to feel terrible

and so we let ourselves
start to forget. That must be it.

Why else would we let the drawbridge
down for a new army, water

the Horseman of Famine's red steed
with the last bucket from the well

or worse—give up then. A heart
sorrow-whipped and cowering

will still nose its ribcage to be petted.
Will still have an urge for heroics.

And anyway, when has fear of grief
actually kept anyone from harm.

Some hope rustles in my leaves
again. It blows through, they eddy

the floor of me, unsettling
all I tried to learn to settle for.

Would I be wiser to keep
a past sacrament folded in my lap

or would I be more wise to shake
the gathered poppies from my apron,

brush off soft crimson petals
of memory and be un-haunted—

I don't know. So I choose you and we
will have to live this to learn what happens.

And though it's tempting to mistake
for wonders the surge of dappled

white-tailed does vaulting through
suburban sliding glass doors,

they are not. Not vanishing bees
blown out like so many thousands

of tiny candle-flames, neither
the glinting throngs of small black birds

suddenly spiraling out of the sky,
the earth almost not even dimpling

with the soft thuds of feathered weight.
Nor the great wet sacks of whale

allowing the tide to deposit them alive
on a strand, nor even the sudden

translucent bloom of jellyfishes.
They're not wonders, but signs

and therefore can be read. I didn't
always know that apocalypse

meant not the end of the world but
the universe disclosing its knowledge

as the sea is meant to give up its dead,
the big reveal, when the veil blows back

like so many cobwebs amid the ruins
and all the meaning of all the evidence

will shine in us to finally see—
And there you'll be and I'll know you

not by the moon in your voice but the song
rung in my animal self. For I feel you,

my sure-handed one, with something
sacreder than instinct but just as fanged.

Then unfold me the way you know
I want so I can watch the stars

blink back on over the garden as we grapple
in the dimming black like little, little gods.

from *Southern Indiana Review*

The S in "I Loves You, Porgy"

◊　◊　◊

makes me think plurality. Maybe I can love you
with many selves. Or. I love all the Porgys.
Even as a colloquialism: a queering of
love as singular. English is a strange
language because I loves
and He loves are not
both grammarly. I loves you,
Porgy. Better to ask what man is not,
Porgy.
The beauty of Nina's Porgy distorts
gravity. Don't let him take
me. The ceiling is in
the floor. There is one name
I cannot say.
Who is

———————

now?
Beauty, a proposal on
refuse. Disposal.
Nina's eyes know
a fist too well. Not
well enough.
Pick one
out a
lineup.

from Poem-a-Day

Hair

◇   ◇   ◇

In the old days
hair was magical.
If hair was cut
you had to make sure it didn't end up
in the wrong hands.

Bad people could mix it
with, say, the spit of a frog.
Or with the urine of a rat!
And certain words
might be spoken.
Then horrible things
might happen to you.

A woman with a husband
in the Navy
could not comb her hair after dark.
His ship might go down.

But good things
could happen, too.
My grandmother
threw a lock of her hair
into the fireplace.
It burned brightly.
That is why she lived
to be a hundred and one.

My uncle had red hair.
One day it started falling out.
A few days later
his infant son died.

Some women let their hair grow long.
If it fell below the knees
that meant
they would never find a husband.

Braiding hair into cornrows
was a safety measure.
It would keep hair
from falling out.

My aunt dropped a hairpin.
It meant somebody
was talking about her.

Birds gathered human hair
to build their nests.
They wove it around sticks.
And nothing happened to the birds.

They were lucky.
But people?

from *The New Yorker*

At Land's End

◊　◊　◊

This garden, its descendants of Stanley's anemones,
flowing, pearlescent like the nacre of shells,

their offspring mine now, in my yard, fragile
beside the orange blare of Dugan's trumpet vine—

the garden's almanac of inheritances swanning
around the bee balm and butterfly bush,

monarchs and black swallowtails fluttering,
a sunflower bowing its great human head

toward the sun. The garden's heart, the lilies,
its consoling perfumes, the *richesse* of memory . . .

What would they say today, I wonder, our Old Ones—

Stanley, ancient and clear-eyed, ready to jump into action,
and Dugan, irascible, a furious activism far in his past,

removed, really, past caring about much—
yet somehow bracing, abrasive.

Their—our—century long over, and today's news—
preposterous—still somehow *unthinkable*:

a barbaric clown "at the helm," breaking
the toys of the circus he never liked anyway—

every treasure, every human pact,
tossed aside as if they were made to be broken.

Playthings of the world, mortal, uprooted.

Oh, Stanley, tending your cultivated dune
under the sun of justice, wiry, undefeated, feeding

your annual seedlings. One late afternoon
long ago, a little too early for martinis,

you lay down your clippers on warm flagstone
by a withering clutch of weeds—

Gail, you said, grabbing my wrist, urgent,
What are we going to do about Bosnia?

Where did it come from, where does it go, that sense of agency?

You, so ready to drop your tools, compost the cuttings,
compost your newspapers for the garden's future—

The Times, The Globe—

as if here at land's end, here on the coast, urgent,
together we'd have energies to do battle forever.

As if we could rescue the guttering world. . . .

from *Salamander*

SHANE McCRAE

The President Visits the Storm

◇   ◇   ◇

"What a crowd! What a turnout!"
—Donald Trump, to victims of Hurricane Harvey

America you're what a turnout great

Crowd a great crowd big   smiles America

The hurricane is everywhere   but here an

Important man is talking here   Ameri-

ca the important president is talking

And if the heavens open up the heavens

Open above the president   the heavens

Open to assume him bodily into heaven

As they have opened to assume great men

Who will come back   and bring the end with them

America he   trumpets the end   of your

Suffering both swan   and horseman trumpeting

From the back of the beast the fire and rose are one

On the president's bright head   the flames implanted

To make a gilded crown America

The hurricane is everywhere   but here

America a great man is a poison

That kills the sky the weather in the sky

For who America   can look above him

You're what a great a crowd big smiles the ratings

The body   of a storm is a man's body

It has an eye and everything in the eye

Is dead   a calm   man is a man who has

Let weakness overcome his urge for death

America the president is talking

You're what a great a turnout   you could be

Anywhere but your anywhere is here

And every inch   of the stadium except those

Feet occupied by the stage   after his speech will

Be used to shelter those displaced by the storm

Except those feet   occupied by the they're

Armed folks   police assigned to guard the stage

Which must remain in place for the duration

Of the hurricane except those feet   of dead

Unmarked space   called *The Safety Zone* between

Those officers and you   you must not vi-
olate *The Safety Zone* you must not leave
The Safety Zone the   president suggests
You find the edge   it's at a common   sense
Distance it is   farther than you can throw

A rock   no farther than a bullet flies

from *Iowa Review*

Bio from a Parallel World

◇   ◇   ◇

Jeffrey McDaniel lives in a small apartment
in Philadelphia. His hair gathered back

into a ponytail. His smile a wobbly
merry-go-round that he hopes you will get on.

He treads water in the same dive bar
every Thursday night. He smiles at each girl

who stumbles in and says, *Would you like to ride
the Tilt-a-Whirl?* Notice how each one of his teeth

is a different shade of yellow. Then he flutters
into the bathroom and digs a roller coaster

out of his pocket. Jeffrey McDaniel inherited
a lot of breadsticks when he was twelve

from his dead grandfather. He has a fake shrine
in his backyard. Sometimes his brothers call him

and ask to borrow lawn furniture. In his pocket,
the calls go to voicemail: *Hi there,*

you sexy little dumpling. Welcome to my earlobe.
Please breathe hard into the mouthpiece. Jeffrey McDaniel

runs his hands along the two *f*'s in his name
like elephant tusks and shakes his head like a bucket

full of soggy trademarks, then he stomps out
of the bathroom and finds a pool of bourbon

hovering near his stool. Girls he knew in college
lounge in bathing suits. He yanks off his t-shirt,

struts out onto the diving board and cannonballs
into his future, which smells just like his past.

from *The Southampton Review*

Miles Davis:
Birth of the Cool/
The Founding of Brasilia
(1950)

◊   ◊   ◊

This is the birth of the cool, atom in the molecule,
raindrop in the storm cloud and child in the man,
this is kind of blue and bitches brew, purity and fusion,
the gesture, the line, arpeggio and appoggiatura,
notes and scales and all the imperial flourishes

this is the plains before Carthage sewn with salt,
the past itself disgraced by the ferocity of the new,
this is the creation of a city in the jungle by a man
with a horn, the founding of a capital and a nation
triumphal boulevards clawed from flowers,

this is the American Song Book harpooned like Moby Dick,
this is the white whale, the white line, the white monster
even Miles cannot over-master,

this is a rainy night in Detroit when Miles walks in
dripping wet, trumpet wrapped in a paper bag,
and starts to play "My Funny Valentine" while the band
on stage is playing "Sweet Georgia Brown,"

I will build your city, I will make the towers rise,
I will raze the jungle and delineate the plazas,
like this, in G, like this, in F sharp,
born a man to raise from the darkness
the artifice of mankind, the symphony which is a city
which is a hive and a bass line and ride cymbal
and a solo cool as polar iron, this is time's bulldozer
clearing a space for the invisible song of the machine,
invisible smoke rising from brush fires and funeral pyres,
I will build Brasilia, I will tame your Amazon,
I will build your mother-fucking city—
here it is, shut up and listen.

from *Salmagundi*

ANGE MLINKO

Sleepwalking in Venice

◇ ◇ ◇

"Two kinds of imagination:
the strong, the promiscuous."
—Leopardi

Calle Rombiasio

Watching a boneless nymph's
half-hearted resurrection
from a spout in the pavement
over and over; catching a glimpse
of the source of my exhaustion,
as if my gaze all this time had lent

muscular support to her effort . . .
She wasn't at all as mischievous
as her sisters, who seeped up
through the flagstones of the court,
serving the blue basilica to us
repurposed as a teacup.

Nor was she splenetic as
the poltergeist in the moka pot,
seething liquid from every fissure,
then exploding on its ring of gas.
If it seemed that water was fraught
with divinities under pressure,

maybe I was going mad myself,
just a little, in this hall of mirrors.
So much glass my eyes glazed over,
and green waves laminating a shelf
where recto sits, and verso appears
in blinding dazzle seeking cover.

Such a surplus of marble that
even in the apartment I occupied
(no palazzo), the stairs luminesced;
if, as Michelangelo had thought,
therein lurked an angel, it was mortified
under the tread of a houseguest.

But when I reached the door,
sprung the lock, climbed the last
spiral flight in thin air,
it was to a wheelhouse (more
or less) of a vessel held fast
to its view of the *sestiere*;

and I was alone with the seagulls,
listening to the creaking ropes
of dinghies below, whose sway
I felt—impossibly—in lulls
unaddressed as sails, or hopes:
tethered to my getaway.

San Marco

Morning glory folded in the scrolls
of columns dissolved their claims
to mass in a bisque-blue apparition;
dusk would blur the ink on rolls
recording their angelic names:
Fra Lippo Lapis, Azure-Titian . . .
like the boaters with their poles,
and not unlike the playground games

where you sidestep the cracks,
or leapfrog stepping-stones,
I tested substantiality bit by bit
with my whole body. Bones
of the duomo melt; how stacks
my hazy realness against it?

Scala d'Oro

I climbed the Golden Staircase.
Hadn't meant to. Who sightsees
council chambers? . . . Blasé
toward doge, lawyer and delegate,
the scoop of whispering galleries,
I was arrested by the gilded vault
where images of Venus and her cult
were preamble to affairs of state.

Head tipped back, hand gripping rail. . . .
I was bowled over by the hubris.
Reached the antechamber reeling
at what hung in the balance: pale
throats bared, a puff piece
for the ages floating on the ceiling.

Antechamber, Main Hall

It struck me that there'd been a fire
in these rooms, if not a brawl.
More *scuro* than *chiaro* in the employ
of the magistrates, choirs
of angels boiled up to forestall
their double-dealings with *trompe l'oeil.*
Sooty gold-and-black marble conspires
to churn an atmosphere of upheaval . . .

Yes, this place was unwholesome.
I made out Hera gifting a peacock

to the republic. Her crowded bower
jostled, unanchored the gaze from
any mooring, put the whole baroque
in service to the reigning power.

Compass Room

"Imagine me as a three-dimensional chessboard
on which several dozen games are being played
around the clock, with multiple figures
whose functions take some up and down the board,
unconstrained by distances; others are confined to diagonals;
and some are either on foot or afloat but never both,
who rest in velvet-lined beds after harlequin day,
a moonlit sapphire set in windows nightly. . . .

"A room sighs when a door is opened, then closed.
I have hoarded all the thieves, swindlers, and traitors
in my iron stanzas like a bank vault, on the understanding
that a productive interest grows in the smallest cell;
that iniquity builds under pressure, from a principal;
that to someone powerful somewhere this is valuable."

Piazzetta

Canal steps troubled by centuries
and off-the-shoulder things
that scandalize the sanctuaries
lead, among the stony echoings,
to wisdom like: *Never send an email*
when you're angry—and never
make a promise when you're happy. (Male
faces grinned.) *We should endeavor,*

one girl submitted, *to take a grain of salt*
with the outburst, the promise made in bed . . .
We should be trained to doubt; the default

will always be ardor. The cafés fed
their chatter into a cochlear gestalt,
a labyrinthine ear with no thread.

Vaporetto

No bellboys, no bellboys, I thought,
bumping the suitcase on each step,
not like Aschenbach had (what had I brought?
my hand squeezed bloodless by the strap).
And having failed to tip and fall,
I gave a last heave, and pushed the thing . . .
it snapped open like an arsenal
of folded silks (for parachute landing

in the dark, with flare). . . . Meanwhile
the bell-buoys in the lagoon recorded data
regarding tides, temperature, salinity,
the migratory sands . . . and if a regatta
glanced off a satellite into infinity,
it hung like a chandelier in time's exile.

Envoi

She turned her ankle playing tennis
ten days before she was to go
on her first, lamentably shelved,
trip to Venice. How then is
she so long and so slow
to make amends to herself? . . .

Stepping back through the looking glass,
I'd tell my friends about the time
I made reservations for Venice,
then had to call them off seeing as
I couldn't negotiate its sublime
on crutches, after a bout of tennis

on an uneven Moroccan clay court
put my right ankle in a cast.
The rhyme surely made an imprecation,
a sort of curse-cum-tort,
as well as the fact that in contrast
to the sport, Venice is a game for one.

The stamp of the real authenticates
imagination's passport, I thought.
Yet as the train drew me backward
across the lagoon (whose cognates
include *lacuna*, of course), I fought
the cold, green voice that declared

It was as though she'd never been.
Yes? *Or it's that she went alone . . .*
and saw myself reflected nowhere,
deprived of some . . . vitamin . . .
like a vampire feeling her bones
that can't find herself in a mirror. . . .

But did she (a funny thing to ask)
sleep deeply, as I see she dreamed well?
I know mon ange—her elaborate schemes;
and in the city of the erotic masque,
her blindfolds and foam plugs are farcical;
bat-spread blackout curtains figure in regimes

where a plan of action or program
to lose consciousness is no paradox.
Refrigeration, wrapped in a duvet, is ideal. . . .
The light doze ends at 1 AM—
an existential cry from the clocks,
the gulling of a campanile.

from *The Paris Review*

Fannie Lou Hamer

◇ ◇ ◇

"I'm sick and tired of being sick and tired!"

She sat across the desk from me, squirming.
It was stifling. My suite runs hot
but most days it is bearable.

This student has turned in nothing,
rarely comes to class. When she does,
her eyes bore into me with a disdain
born long before either of us.

She doesn't trust anything I say.
She can't respect my station,
the words coming out of these lips,
this face. My breathing
is an affront. *It's me*, she says.

I never was this student's professor—
her immediate reaction
seeing me at the Smart Board.
But I have a calling to complete
& she has to finish college,
return to a town where
she doesn't have to look at,
listen to or respect anyone
like me—forever tall, large
& brown in her dagger eyes,
though it's clear she looks down
on me. She can return—

if not to her hometown, another
enclave, so many others, where
she can brush a dog's golden coat,
be vegan & call herself
a good person.

Are you having difficulty with your other classes?

No.

Go, I say, tenderly.

Loaded as a cop's gun,
she blurts point-blank
that she's *afraid* of me. Twice.
My soft syllables rattle something
planted deep,
so I tell her to go where
she'd feel more comfortable
as if she were my niece or
godchild, even wish her
a good day.

If she stays, the ways
this could backfire!
Where is my Kevlar shield
from her shame?

There's no way to tell
when these breasts will evoke
solace or terror. I hate
that she surprises me, that I lull
myself to think her ilk
is gone despite knowing
so much more, and better.

I can't proselytize my worth
all semester, exhaust us
for the greater good.
I can't let her make me

a monster to myself—
I'm running out of time & pity
the extent of her impoverished
heart. She's from New
England, I'm from the Mid-South.
Far from elderly, someone
just raised her like this
with love.

I have essays to grade
but words warp
on the white page, dart
just out of reach. I blink
two hours away, find it hard
to lift my legs, my voice,
my head precious to my parents
now being held
in my own hands.

How did they survive
so much worse, the millions
with all of their scars!
What would these rivers be
without their weeping,
these streets without
their faith & sweat?

Fannie Lou Hamer
thundered what they felt,
we feel, into DNC microphones
on black-and-white TV
years before
I was a notion.

She doesn't know who
Fannie Lou Hamer is,
and never has to.

from Poem-a-Day

The Last of England

◇   ◇   ◇

Three o'clock in the morning
      in this hotel whose name
            I cannot remember.

Am I screaming now
            am I making any sound at all?

Concentrate   Andrew.

Imagine tomorrow.

Imagine dozens of knives and forks
      in kitchen drawers
            lined with soft green baize.

Imagine
      the shoe-shine boy
            already skimming his tin of polish
      and row of new-laid eggs
            waiting at room temperature.

But still the ship will not sail
      the glittery liner whose name
            will come to me in a moment.

Still it is
      moored to the solid earth.

Bound to the stifling earth
    while vast wheels of stars
        continue to spin overhead

and dawn
    refuses to meet the horizon.

from *The American Scholar*

Aubade

◇ ◇ ◇

At 1 a.m. the dairy sink
in your yard was a deer-glyphed megalith
caught in my headlights.
I found not only sermons
in stones but Tamerlane of Samarkand
in the Timberland mukluks
tossed on your bedroom floor.
Now I'd rather shop for staples
(bread, milk, Clorox)
at the twenty-four-hour Supermart
than lag
behind the laggard
dawn about to steal
from haystack to haystack, no less bent

on taking us to the brink
of destruction than was Clement V
on the Knights
Templar. He was determined
to disband
that herd of ten-point bucks
by showing them the door
courtesy of a papal
bull he dubbed "Vox
in excelso." For I'm averse, sweetheart,
to ever again seeing a stag
take the head staggers,
ever again seeing dawn kneel
as if it might repent,

as if it might come to think
of itself as a figure from some ancient myth—
Mesopotamian? Hittite?
Greek? German?—
throwing up its hands
with the dumbstruck
oaks or shaking to their cores
the Japanese maples,
unyoking the great ox
from the straw-laden cart
even as it divines the hag
in the haggard,
then putting its shoulder to the wheel
it means to reinvent.

from *The New Yorker*

On Confessionalism

◇   ◇   ◇

Not sleepwalking, but waking still,
   with my hand on a gun, and the gun
in a mouth, and the mouth
   on the face of a man on his knees.
Autumn of '89, and I'm standing
   in a section 8 apartment parking lot,
pistol cocked, and staring down
   at this man, then up into the mug
of an old woman staring, watering
   the single sad flower to the left
of her stoop, the flower also staring.
   My engine idling behind me, a slow
moaning bassline and the bark
   of a dead rapper nudging me on.
All to say, someone's brokenhearted.
   And this man with the gun in his mouth—
this man who, like me, is really little
   more than a boy—may or may not
have something to do with it.
   May or may not have said a thing
or two, betrayed a secret, say,
   that walked my love away. And why
not say it: She adored me. And I,
   her. More than anyone, anything
in life, up to then, and then still,
   for two decades after. And, therefore,
went for broke. Blacked out and woke
   having gutted my piggy and pawned

all my gold to buy what a homeboy
    said was a Beretta. Blacked out
and woke, my hand on a gun, the gun
    in a mouth, a man, who was really
a boy, on his knees. And because
    I loved the girl, I actually paused
before I pulled the trigger—once,
    twice, three times—then panicked
not just because the gun jammed,
    but because what if it hadn't,
because who did I almost become,
    there, that afternoon, in a section 8
apartment parking lot, pistol cocked,
    with the sad flower staring, because
I knew the girl I loved—no matter
    how this all played out—would never
have me back. Day of damaged ammo,
    or grime that clogged the chamber.
Day of faulty rods, or springs come
    loose in my fist. Day nobody died,
so why not *hallelujah*? Say *amen* or
    Thank you? My mother sang for years
of God, babes and fools. My father,
    lymph node masses fading from
his X-rays, said surviving one thing
    means another comes and kills you.
He's dead, and so, I trust him. Dead,
    and so I'd wonder, years, about the work
I left undone—boy on his knees
    a man now, risen, and likely plotting
his long way back to me. Fuck it.
    I tucked my tool like the movie gangsters
do, and jumped back in my bucket.
    Cold enough day to make a young man
weep, afternoon when everything,
    or nothing, changed forever. The dead
rapper grunted, the bassline faded,
    my spirits whispered something
from the trees. I left, then lost the pistol

in a storm drain, somewhere between
that life and this. Left the pistol in
    a storm drain, but never got around
to wiping away the prints.

            from *The Common*

You Are Your Own State Department

◇ ◇ ◇

Each day I miss Japanese precision. Trying to arrange things
   the way they would. I miss the call to prayer
at Sharjah, the large collective pause. Or
the shy strawberry vendor with rickety wooden cart,
single small lightbulb pointed at a mound of berries?
   In one of China's great cities, before dawn.

   Forever I miss my Arab father's way with mint leaves
      floating in a cup of sugared tea—his delicate hands
arranging rinsed figs on a plate. What have we here?
   said the wolf in the children's story
stumbling upon people doing kind, small things.
   Is this small monster one of us?

When your country does not feel cozy, what do you do?
   Teresa walks more now, to feel closer to her
ground. If destination within two miles, she must
hike or take the bus. Carries apples,
   extra bottles of chilled water to give away.
      Kim makes one positive move a day for someone else.

I'm reading letters the ancestors wrote after arriving

    in the land of freedom, words in perfect English script . . .

describing gifts they gave one another for Christmas.

   Even the listing seems oddly civilized,

these 1906 Germans . . . *hand-stitched embroideries for dresser*

tops. Bow ties. Slippers, parlor croquet, gold ring, "pretty

    inkwell."

How they comforted themselves! A giant roast

   made them feel more at home.

    Posthumous medals of honor for

coming, continuing—could we do that?

And where would we go?

    My father's hope for Palestine

stitching my bones, "no one wakes up and

    dreams of fighting around the house"—

someday soon the steady eyes of children in Gaza,

   yearning for a little extra electricity

to cool their lemons and cantaloupes, will be known.

     Yes?

   We talked for two hours via Google Chat,

they did not complain once. Discussing stories,

   books, families, a character who does

     what you might do.

Meanwhile secret diplomats are what we must be,

   as a girl in Qatar once assured me,

    each day slipping its blank visa into our hands.

      from *Fifth Wednesday*

Rasputin Aria

◇　◇　◇

I wish I did not think of Rasputin
so often. To have been born with a penis which in
manhood would be said to be,
erect, 14" long,
some said 18"
organ which he used in brutal
acts, penetrating helplessness,
and then, at the end of his life, to be taken
from behind, raped, then castrated,
penis and testicles, harps of the nerves,
gone—and then to be killed one way,
and it did not take, and then another,
then stabbed and drowned in a sack—
though all that was found was the skein of burlap
bitten and torn open and washed up—
a cruel male leader, a brigand,
law unto himself, taken, the shock of it, the
disbelief, the poor anus from the
worldwide family of anuses,
the species's helpless O, and the poor
penis, brother to the poor sister
vagina—tis of thee I think
when I think of my country rendering,
and being rendered, when I think of our body
politic, its head of wrath
with an orange flame for hair.

from *The Southampton Review*

Nord-Sud

◊　◊　◊

That day when I thought of Pierre Reverdy
for the first and final time

I counted the butterflies in Rome.
In Rome I counted the butterflies.

There were always three,
three on Trajan's blood-stained column,

three within the Memoirs of Hadrian,
three alight on the Virgin's left thigh,

three perched amidst the eternal dust.
(I counted to three because I felt I must.)

Electric blue were these creatures of air
born of the mind of Pierre Reverdy

mourning the death of a violin by fire.
The Tiber is flowing somewhat lazily today

past a distant echo of Pierre Reverdy,
past the burning manuscripts of Pierre Reverdy

lighting the banks not of Tiber but of Seine.
I counted the butterflies in Paris then

as they caught fire one by one,
one by a lock at the Quai de Valmy,

one by the dying guillotine
on the Place de la Cloche Vide

where three last songs could be heard.
You waved graciously and sang along

as poetry, that blind ballerina in flames,
bid you farewell while taking one last bow

with no regrets other than a few.
The earth is perfectly still

and the butterflies have ended their day
in the north and in the south.

Listen, Pierre, the hands on the clock
point towards the snows of yesteryear.

Pierre, you died as we were about to meet.
This poem is to be continued indefinitely.

from *Harper's*

The Black Saint
& The Sinner Lady
& The Dead & The Truth

◇ ◇ ◇

For one thing, I hate stillness. On the front porch,
waiting, I see an animal I don't recognize:

feet of a bird, wings of a leaf. The grotesqueness
of attachment, the loudness of the woods, I knew it

when I was dead before. I died for my sins
and because of this, I am in the woods now,

aching. It is June. I am used to being
a certain kind of alone. Soon my photosynthesis

will be complete, and I will be the gap
between Angela Davis's teeth. Do you ever

love something so much, you become it?
Like how when hard rain comes, you learn

quick. You straighten your shoulders and hope
this is better than touching.

I say *casual death*, and the half-moon
is my enemy, an uncertain white girl.

I wish I didn't care. I am myself
shaking hands, so subtle no one notices.

Sometimes, it's my ribcage, or my throat
does the same damn thing as my skull,

the little bear inside it. Please
don't make me repeat myself.

from *Harper's*

Head Crack Head Crack

◇　◇　◇

Zoo Bang
Auld Lang

Brick City
Fly Ditty

Drug War
Street Noir

War Fat
Bank That

Sneaker Box
Check Account

Get Fresh
Stay Fly

Night Pool
Old School

Stash House
Corner Store

We Cool
No More

Smoked Out
Player's Ball

Okey Doke
Flat Broke

Hang Out
No Doubt

Black Out
Death Count

Dwight Gone
Tone Gone

Petey Gone
Chino Gone

Body Shot
Chop Shop

Black Hole
Myths Sold

Break That
Like This

Black Cat
Death Kiss

Power Move
Move That

Krush Groove
Dope Shit

Step Back
Get This

from *Green Mountains Review*

Star Map
with Action Figures

◇   ◇   ◇

More dark than gray, but not yet quite dark
entirely, the stories keep ending as if there were
a limit to what any story could hold onto, and this
the limit, the latest version of it, looking a lot like the sea
meeting shore.

★

To constellate, the way desire
does, sometimes, with fear, or anger—both, occasionally—
and there's been gentleness, too, *I'm here, I've*
always been here . . .

★

Maybe between mystery
and what little we can say for sure
happened, lies a secret even
memory itself keeps somewhere
hidden because for now
it has to.

★

Less like wishing too late, I mean,
for a thing to be otherwise than like fire closing in

so absolutely, it can almost seem intimacy
had yet to be invented, and here's the fire,
inventing it: *Constellate,*
with me—

★

      Look at the field,
studded with the blue-black eyes of broken heroes.
One of the eyes is moving. It can still see. What does it see?

from *Virginia Quarterly Review*

Just Rollin' Along

◊ ◊ ◊

Louis Charles (L. C. "Good Rockin'" Robinson (born Louis Charles Robinson; May 13, 1914–September 26, 1976) was an American blues singer, guitarist, and fiddle player. "He played an electric steel guitar. Robinson was more than just a storyteller. He was one of the Bay Area's most significant blues artists, . . . who helped shape what's come to be known as West Coast Blues. When Robinson died in 1976, [Ron] Steward recounts, the influential bluesman was near penniless and friends had to pass a hat around at his funeral."

—Jim Harrington

It was '34 Oklahoma and L.C. was doing a gig
People were doing the Texas Two Step
And greasing on the pig
There were mounds upon mounds of ice cream
The pies were crusty and fine
The following story is true and I ain't lyin'
Good Rockin' Robinson was packing them in
But the noise of a Ford sedan disrupted the
Din
A woman and a man
The man had a grin

They were
Just rollin' along
Just rollin' along

Her lap held a Thompson
The barrel was long
"I'll give you 12 silver dollars," she said
"If you play our song"
"I'm sitting on top of the world"
"I'm sitting on top of the world"

They were Just rollin' along
Just rollin' along

They paid Good Rockin' and
Were on their way
Very few in the crowd will forget that
Day
The policeman pulled up
He was all out of breath
"Did you see a couple in a Ford
Come this way?
She was dapper," he said
"He wore a Newsboy cap
And a pistol on his side"

Good Rockin' asked who was
In that ride
The policeman said
"It was Bonnie and Clyde"
The policeman said
"It was Bonnie and Clyde"

They were
Just rollin' along
Just rollin' along

from *Black Renaissance Noire*

Four Marys

◇   ◇   ◇

—*Madonna del Parto*, 1460, Piero della Francesca

Are the drapes drawn open, or being closed?
Each of the heavy, velvet wings is clasped
in the hands of a little angel, a little man really,
in shades of plum and mint green that frame
the birthing tent's opening for a girl
who retreats into or emerges from the dark.
It isn't clear: the perspective is such
that if I cover the painting's
top half with a hand, Mary steps forward;
if I cover the lower, she shrinks back,
her blue bodice split at the bulging seams
to show the pear-white cut of her linen shift,
the great weight of the child she is about to bear
and later bury. And even if I didn't believe
the child would rise again, I would believe the artist
had seen such fear paint a girl's face
when the eldest women in the village
are called for help, and fresh straw brought in
if there isn't a bed, and hot water, and rose oil to rub
over the hips, and vinegar and sugar water
to drink, and hog's gut and a thick needle
to sew her up with later. Even if I did not believe
in Mary's joy, I would believe in her pain, the quick flick
of her thoughts turning to the sister, or the cousin,
or to her own mother who died giving birth,
the baby too not making it, for the birth

was in winter: ice so clogged the village's
deep ruts that the midwife's cart slipped
into the soak dike, splitting the wood wheel
in two, and by the time the woman could walk
the steep hill up to the villa, the mother had torn,
and in the rush to save her, no one worked
quick enough to cut the cord wrapped
around the baby's throat. Or the baby came out
strong and fine, but died two years later
when it stumbled into a fire, or was bitten by a rat
and sickened and starved, or caught the fever
that spread through town when all the animals
were stabled inside the houses for winter.
So many people died, so many people
were supposed to die, it's hard to conceive
of how the mothers survived their grief,
and how they named their next, living baby
after the dead one, because the name, at least,
was good. It's hard to know if I should read
the deepest grief or resignation or both in the line
from Mary Shelley's 1818 notebook, the year
her daughter, Clara, died, two weeks
after Mary had given birth to her. *Woke this morning.*
Found my baby dead, all the little black scratching pen
could add to paper, and the rest was blank,
and then there were months, and then
there was *Frankenstein*. Piero della Francesca
painted an embroidery of pomegranates
into Mary's birthing tent, symbol of fruitfulness
and of the underworld, of a mother's grief
and of her rage to get her child back, the daughter
both dead and alive to her, as Mary knows her own child
is both dead and alive to us. A winter fruit
for the winter birth of a rich woman
whose house wanted to ward off a grueling
delivery, and so whose midwife would feed her
pomegranate seeds to sustain her, a fruit
the midwife herself would eat only once, as payment
from the duke for the son she finally ushered

for him into the world. Such a strange, leathery
skin, though the color was bright
as blood on fresh linen, and who could have expected
those glistening cells packed inside, wet prisms
in the ruby eye of a ruby insect, or the heart
of a god who takes what he wants
and never gives it back. The midwife took the fruit home
and split it with her husband, and tried not to think
of the bed of the girl she'd just left, its stains
that looked almost black in the dawn light,
and how the girl's skin had turned bluish, the fragile spring
she'd require to spend alone in bed away from the duke
and healing. How can Mary not look
downcast before these curtains that threaten
to close on her, to open? *I have no doubt
of seeing the animal today*, Mary Wollstonecraft
Godwin, Mary Shelley's mother wrote,
meaning birth, meaning Mary, the little animal
she never saw grow up, because Wollstonecraft
died of an infection days after giving birth.
But before that was told she could not nurse
her infant daughter for fear the corruption
would spread through her milk, though she stayed
at Mary's bedside the final three days of her life.
And Godwin beside her, who, because he loved
his wife, believed her genius could survive
any truth, and so published a memoir later
detailing everything: Wollstonecraft's affairs,
her daughter's illegitimacy, attempts at suicide, so that
in 1798 the index of the *Anti-Jacobin Review* would publish,
under the heading "Prostitution," *See Mary
Wollstonecraft.* Two towns over from his Madonna,
in a church in Arezzo, Piero della Francesca
painted a fresco of Mary Magdalene, her curled hair wet
with the tears she used to bathe Christ's feet,
her body a swollen green swathe of dress, the red cape
folded so as to accentuate the pendulous belly
and thick thigh, the Magdalene bristling
between arch columns that frame her, one

painted slightly forward, the other behind
her body, so that we do not know in which direction
Mary is headed, nor what she is, really,
her almond eyes glittering out at us, halo chipped,
over centuries, away. It is wonderful
when time accentuates something of the truth
already within us: the frank look, the unabashed
leg with which the woman kicks off the covers from the bed
of the man to whom she is not married; the neat,
round muscle of his shoulder pressed against hers
in the dark, his body over and over coming alive
under her hands, a dream or a nightmare
Mary Shelley once had of Clara.
All this time, she told her husband, their daughter
had not been dead at all, only cold, the little body frozen
and waiting to be attended to. *And so we rubbed
it before the fire, and now it lives,* she told
Shelley in the conversation recorded
in her journal, and cried awhile, and went to bed.
Then woke again the next morning, and remembered.
The midwife, walking back down from the villa
three summers later, having attended the birth
of the duke's new, less delicate wife, hums a song
to herself that she hummed to the baby
she just left, a girl this time, no pomegranates
for payment; a girl who will, if lucky, inherit
her mother's strength and her plainness, both traits
the midwife believes might protect her from
and in the birthing bed. She'll grow up,
the midwife thinks, and marry, and have children
herself, some less or more like her, sons
with obdurate natures, perhaps, or a daughter
who inherits her curly hair, perhaps the sturdy thighs
of a woman like this shopkeeper kneeling now by a store
in the Piazza Grande to retrieve a shower of euros
from someone's coin purse. The woman stands, straightens,
and I see her mouth thin to a not unpleasant line
as she looks out at me, calculating, perhaps,
the time until lunch as she tugs at the waist

of her linen pants. The yellow pleats sag, slack
at her belly. The weight from a pregnancy
she never lost, perhaps, or the thickening
that comes to anyone, in the later part of life.

from *AGNI*

SONIA SANCHEZ

Belly, Buttocks,
and Straight Spines

◊   ◊   ◊

for Sister Wangechi Mutu

(1)

you—enigmatic woman exploding
from clouds and intestines, riverbanks,
kneecaps, veins and horizons
tongues embroidered with eyelashes.

you burn in my throat
i walk your footsteps
singing.

       you are here. you are there.
you will never go away.
you kiss your own breath
sleepwalk your eyes
stretch out with moths
singing your legs.

(2)

i know your butterfly sweet
your lips taste of the sea
the years dusty with herstory
anticipate light.

your hands riot with pain
collapse in new prayer
touch this western stained
glass where ghosts commit
themselves to military blood.

the bleating hips
surrounding your teeth
wrapped in laughter
blood laughter
brittle noise
seaweed souls
whistling words

whose lil pumpkin are you?
who is your sister?
where is your mama?
our thumbs bleed ashes.
in this travel dust bowl.

(3)

this is a blues sermon
i think, hanging from
the sky
scratching at the night
where literary brains
demystify deaths.
seen from the angle
of your life,
you turn at the waist
in red and purple confetti
the day stitches up
your python mouth.

you stroll black
beyond the stars
star leaping blk/skinned
woman

seen from the angle
of the camera, you become
the mug shot
mugging a century of
incestuous nipples.
sounds . . . video . . . smell . . .
riding death on
its lens
do not feed the animals
they will bite one day.

who speaks
who has spoken
this squat language
where are the vowels
and consonants and diphthongs?
do not feed the animals
they squat in herds
and will bite one day . . .

(4)

red orange breasts
leaking medical
hieroglyphics
bones for sale
immaculate bones for sale

stage right:

Ethiopian bodies
leaking into the ground

                                  stage left:

old clothes unburied
children's eyes undressed
men's pants unzipped
women's slips slipping
standing still backstage
a-waiting modernity
master monsters with batons
conducting infernos

is God calling
your limbs to pray
to prey on

                    what's in a name
a leg, a heart, a skull
an ancestral wind?
your intellect teases us
with zero tolerance for lies.
what's in a kiss? a smell?
a black woman in white chalk?
a woman sleepwalking
on corners?
what is erotic about
a false step?
yo me espero, yo me espero
i wait for my coming, I wait for my coming.

now as your congregational
knees kneel
now that your birth laughs
a long pause
now that you sigh amid
the pale gaze of thirst,
is that God's tongue
sliding down your throat?

      (5)

yo sé, lo sé, yo sé
i know, i know it, i know
where is this brown skinned woman going
with her military hair
a bright hysterical flower
eating cake smiling cake
regurgitating cake
yo sé, lo sé, yo sé
i know, i know it, i know
smell the jelly roll woman
squatting in her skin

her bright face eating bluesorrow
smell the doctoral urgency
of her shudderings
female pain profiling
her hunger.

who scrubs the day white
while women fall down
with crucifixions?
can you hear
their birdspirits
strumming gravity?
can you hear
the saxophone
bloodletting the ghosts shout?
can you play this woman
with your fingers?
can you hear
her confetti feet
dancing undeposited rhythms?

NOW HEAR THIS. NOW HEAR THIS.

harpsichord teeth
mothbred smiles
put vaginas in a pill
box for awhile . . .

telegraphic buttocks
in bathroom stalls
you are tattooed on our eyes
against the tabloid walls . . .

mouths anointed with
peacock pricks hey, hey, hey
here I am, here i am
come along take your pick
hey hey hey hey hey hey

listen. listen. listen . . .

woman of eye socket-bone
love can wear you down
to a spinal eye-bone
love can make you drink
your own blood
lessen you got a catcher's mitt
don't go playing with love. love. blood.

(6)

silence. silence. ma chère
ca ya te. ca ya te. mi amor
no consecrated birthwaters . . . today
no quicksilver blankets . . . today
no surgical procedures . . . today
just Bantu music with an asterick beat . . . today
just a night shudder under your arms . . . today
just a pistol whipped skin . . . today
just a lost pulse beat . . . today
just a railroad train of butts . . . today
just a machete beat against the sky . . . today
just some cocked cocks standing at attention . . . today

listen. listen. listen. Sister Wangechi
you hear me, don't you?
and you hear, don't you, how your
collages dance their amputee delirium.
Sister Wangechi you hear me, don't you
you hear the sacred music
ease-dropping these gallery walls
praising your beauty and bones
in this hallway of lost sermons,
you hear me don't you
you hear the children running
a furious circle of legs
jumping adolescent rhymes
as they light up streets
with garbage bag balls as they

spill their magical spines
their genius, their surplus
knees on streets.

it is evening and we have
arrived in your arms of
lost seconds
you hear me don't you
even as you navigate
this halo of ordained voyages
as you uncork the daylight
past these shadows
past our doors left open
and your gentle breath fills
the day with sweet eyelids
of silver
as you arrive at the arc of your name.
Sister Wangechi Mutu
you hear me, don't you, and
i invoke your name, your
gallery of female matadors
as they come and dance in thunder . . . (click)

from *Valley Voices* and *Black Renaissance Noire*

#MeToo

◇ ◇ ◇

So #MeToo cuts her ponytail off, walks into a bar and takes a seat next to #MeToo and the bartender serves #MeToo whiskey from an eye-dropper she pulls straight out of her purse, but it turns out #MeToo was already in every purse because #MeToo comes as a picture inside every wallet. #MeToo carries tweezers everywhere she goes, plucks chin hairs before her picture is taken. #MeToo slides into a bra strap, tucks into a sock, falls out of a pocket, folds into a shirtsleeve, gets lost in a discount rack. #MeToo Shuts up. Drinks. #MeToo never loses the memory.

#MeToo, like when my high school soccer coach hijacked my shin pads and cleats he drained the water cooler sucked the orange slice out of my mouth the warehouse out of my mind the metal cage out of my lungs the ferris wheel seat that flips inside my gut yes he resigned I was a goalie I wanted to tell his wife wanted to cut his tongue out rip his face off my torso hardened into tree bark when my shirt came off her torso hardened into tree bark when her shirt came off she wanted his wife to yell but it was sunday then tuesday and 16 is hard pavement her head is my head against the curb my hair wrapped around her throat I was 16 I swear I never kissed back

So #MeToo wants to tell his wife, wants his daughter's name not to be Nicole. #MeToo was kicked off the soccer team. He ran for mayor as a democrat, just like #MeToo. So you lost the sour taste of being a teenager, #MeToo? Me too. Now she stands in front of a classroom twenty years later with hair down to her knees and when a student says #MeToo, she imagines her soccer cleats dangling from his rearview mirror as he gags on a wad of her hair.

from *The Seventh Wave*

The Women's March

◇　　◇　　◇

So many mothers are here, daughters and granddaughters.
Mine's been dead for nineteen years but somehow
managed to come. I'm seeing her everywhere,
in the pleased-with-itself smile of the little girl
riding her father's shoulders, holding a sign
announcing girl power and the beginning of the
Women's Century, in the don't-mess-with-me look
of the much-pierced young woman in black
who appears to have finally found her cadence,
in the excited green-gray eyes of the old woman
in a wheelchair being pushed along at quite a clip
by, I assume, her grandson, who looks absolutely
mesmerized. And just ahead is the forceful stride
of the black drummer banging away for all she is
and wants to be, using everything she has to make
a point about strength and willfulness and sacrifice
that maybe only women have the right to make,
having made all of us, shared themselves so completely.
A point about going too far and not far enough,
about time, and the pain it brings, and yes, here I am,
older than I ever intended to be, enjoying the ringing
in my ears, remembering being lifted into the air
by my mother, trembling with joy, as she enfolded
me into the hospitable wings of her peasant apron.
Yes, she's here, marching with all the others, all of whom
understand what's being asked of them, one more time.

from *The Southern Review*

LLOYD SCHWARTZ

Vermeer's Pearl

◊   ◊   ◊

I used to boast that I never lived in a city without a Vermeer.

—You do now, a friend pointed out, when the one Vermeer in my city was stolen.

It's still missing.

The museum displays its empty frame.

But there are eight Vermeers in New York, more than any other city— and not so far away.

Sometimes even more.

Once, the visiting Vermeer was one of his most beloved paintings.

It was even more beautiful than I remembered.

A young girl, wearing a turban of blue and yellow silk, is just turning her face to watch you entering the room.

She seems slightly distracted by someone a little off to your right, maybe someone she knows better than you.

Her mouth is slightly open, as if she's just taken a breath and is about to speak.

The light falling on her is reflected not only on her large pearl earring but also in her large shining eyes ("Those are pearls," sings Ariel of a man drowned in a tempest at sea, "that were his eyes").

And on her moist lips.

There's even a little spot of moisture in a corner of her mouth.

Some art historians think this was not intended to be a portrait, just a study of a figure in an exotic costume.

Yet her presence is so palpable, she seems right there in the room with you, radiating unique and individual life.

Already in the museum is another Vermeer in which a woman writing a letter has a similar pearl earring.

She's interrupted by her maid handing her a letter—is it from the person she's just been writing to?

And in a nearby museum there's a painting of a young woman with piercing eyes and another enormous pearl dangling from her ear (a "teardrop pearl").

She's staring out a window and tuning a lute.

Scholars tell us that these pearls aren't really pearls—no pearl so large has ever come to light.

No oyster could be big enough.

So the famous pearl is probably just glass painted to look like a pearl.

Pearl of no price.

Yet as you look, the illusion of the pearl—the *painted* pearl, glistening, radiant, fragile, but made real by the light it radiates—becomes before your eyes a metaphor for the girl wearing it.

Or if not the girl, then Vermeer's painting of her.

from *Harvard Review*

Encore

◇   ◇   ◇

Cold, that's how I was. I couldn't shake it off, especially
those last days and nights doing all the right things
in the wrong spirit, in the antithesis of spirit, more
machine of son than son, mechanical, efficient, wiping
and cleaning and so having to see and touch what it would have
sickened me to touch and look at if I hadn't left my body
to the automatic pilot of its own devices so I could do
what needed doing inside the deprivation chamber of this final
chapter, which the TV looked out on glumly through game
show, soap, old sappy black-and-white unmastered films.

I was cold all the time, I couldn't shake it off till
I was free of her, however briefly, in the parking lot
or at home for a quick drink or toke, anything
to draw some vestige of fellow feeling out of hiding—
hiding deer-like in a clearing at the end of hunting season,
starved but fearful, warily sniffing the scentless air,
breathing in the fresh absence of her scent too new
too sudden not to be another trap—you're dutiful,
she'd say when I'd come back, as always, I'll give you that.

And I *was* cold: I couldn't help feel there was something
scripted and too rehearsed even about her dying,
laid on too thickly, like a role that every book club
romance, soap, musical and greeting card had been
a training for, role of a lifetime, role "to die for"
and O how she would have played it to the hilt
if not for the cold I couldn't shake—which must have so
enraged her—not my lack of feeling but my flat refusal

to pretend to feel, to play along (was that too much to ask?)
and throw myself into the part so we could both, this once
at least, rise to the occasion of what we never shared.

That final day, for instance, the way the Fighting Sullivans on TV
seemed to watch us watch them as a taunt or dare parade their
small town big war grieving fanfare across the screen,
the five sons killed in battle, only the old man holding back,
not crying when he's told the news, not breaking down or
even touching the wife he still calls mother, a stoicism fraught
with all the feeling he stuffs back down inside him as he grabs
his lunch pail, heads to work, just as he would on any other day,
the only hint of sorrow the salute he gives as the train chugs past
the water tower on the top of which the apparitions of his boys
stand waving calling out goodbye pop, see you round pop—

and as the credits roll she's asking if there's anything, anything
at all about the past, the family, her childhood that I'd like to
hear about before she dies, her voice decked out so gaudily
in matriarchal sweetness that I freeze, I shake my head, say,
no, ma, no, I'm good. And just like that the scene is over,
the sweetness vanishes into the air, into thin air, like the
baseless fabric of the mawkish film, an insubstantial pageant
faded as she nods and grimaces and turns away
relieved (it almost seemed) that that was that. Was us. Was me.
The role that I was born for, and she was done with now.

And yet it's never done, is it. The pageant's never faded.
Shake off the cold and it gets colder. There's just no end
to how cold the cold can get, not even on the coldest nights,
not even if I throw the windows open wide and turn
the ceiling fan on high and lie in bed, uncovered,
naked, shivering inward back into myself as if to draw
the cold in with me deeper, down to the icy center stage
where I will always find her frozen in the act of turning from me
while I stand freezing saying, no, I'm good.

from *The Threepenny Review*

Who Knows One

◇ ◇ ◇

Who knows One. I know One.
One is God for God is One—
The only One in Heaven and on earth.

Who knows two. I know two.
Two are the first two: Adam and Eve.
One is God for God is One—
It takes one to know one.

Who knows three. I know three.
Bad things always come in threes.
Two trees grew in the Garden of Eden.
One is God for God is One—
One rotten apple spoils the barrel.

Who knows four. I know four.
What were you doing on all fours?
Three's the hearts in a *ménage à trois*.
Two's the jump ropes in double Dutch.
One is God for God is One—
One good turn deserves another.

Who knows five. I know five.
Five is the five in *Slaughterhouse-Five*.
Four is Egypt's plague of flies.
Three the Stooges on TV.
Two the two-faced lie he told.
One is God for God is One—
One hand washes the other.

Who knows six. I know six.
Six are the wives of Henry VIII.
Who? What? Where? When? Why?
Four the phases of the moon.
Three the bones inside the ear.
Two eyes—the better to see you with, my dear.
One is God for God is One—
There's only one to a customer.

Who knows seven. I know seven.
Seven the year of the seven-year itch.
Six the paper anniversary.
Asked if he did it, he pleaded the Fifth.
Four are my absent wisdom teeth.
Three is the three in the third degree.
Two can play that game.
One is God for God is One—
Public Enemy No. 1.

Who knows eight. I know eight.
The Beatles' "Eight Days a Week."
Wrath is the seventh of the deadly sins.
Six of one, half a dozen of the other.
He lost it all in five-card stud.
Four bits in a nibble equals half a byte.
Three is the beginning, middle, and end.
Two are the graves in the family plot.
One is God for God is One—
The only one in a hole in one.

Who knows nine. I know nine.
Nine are the lives of an average cat.
Eight is the day of circumcision.
Seven the locks on Samson's head.
Six the sense I wish I had.
Five the five in nickeled-and-dimed.
Four cold feet in the double bed.
Three's a crowd.
Two's company.

One is God for God is One—
The only one in a one-night stand.

Who knows ten. I know ten.
I wouldn't touch that with a ten-foot pole.
She dressed to the nines.
Fellini's *8½*.
Seven the times the bride circles the groom.
Six the number perfect in itself.
She daubed her wrists with Chanel No. 5.
Love is just a four-letter word.
Three is as phony as a three-dollar bill.
Two is the two in doubletalk.
One is God for God is One—
There's one born every minute.

Who knows eleven. I know eleven.
Eleven are the stars in Joseph's dream.
Ten is the Roman Numeral X.
Possession is nine-tenths of the law.
Infinity's a sideways figure eight.
Seven long years Jacob had to wait.
Six is the Lover's Tarot card.
Five is indivisible.
Four, cruel April.
Three witches in the Scottish play.
Two is the two of "I and Thou."
One is God for God is One—
One in the hand is worth two in the bush.

Who knows twelve. I know twelve.
Twelve are the face cards in a deck.
Eleven are the thieves in *Ocean's Eleven*.
Take a deep breath and count to ten.
It takes nine tailors to make a man.
Eight are the people on Noah's ark.
Seven are the hues in a rainbow's arc.
Six is . . . I can't remember what.
Five the rivers of the Underworld.

Four the rivers of Paradise.
Three on a match.
It takes two to tango.
One is God for God is One—
In one ear and out the other.

Who knows thirteen. I know thirteen.
Thirteen is the skyscraper's missing floor.
Twelve are the men who walked on the moon.
At the eleventh hour, his life was spared.
Do not covet your neighbor's ass.
Nine are the circles of Dante's Hell.
Eight is the game of crazy eights.
The phone was busy 24/7.
They deep-sixed their love affair.
The five-o'clock shadow on your face.
Four is putting two and two together.
Three is the eternal triangle.
Two plays second fiddle.
Two minus one equals one.
One is one all alone.
You were my one and only one—
The only one whose number's up.

from *The New Yorker*

The Greatest Personal Privation

◇   ◇   ◇

The greatest personal privation I have had to endure has
been the want of either Patience or Phoebe—tell them I
am never, if life is spared us, to be without both of them
again.
> —letter from Mary Jones to Elizabeth Jones Maxwell
> regarding two of her slaves, 30 August 1849

1.

It is a painful and harassing business
Belonging to her. We have had trouble enough,
Have no comfort or confidence in them,

And they appear unhappy themselves, no doubt
From the trouble they have occasioned.
They could dispose of the whole family

Without consulting us—Father, Mother,
Every good cook, washer, and seamstress
Subject to sale. I believe Good shall be

Glad if we may have hope of the loss of trouble.
I remain in glad conscience, at peace with God
And the world! I have prayed for those people

Many, many, very many times.

2.

Much as I should miss Mother,
I have had trouble enough
And wish no more to be
Only waiting to be sent
Home in peace with God.

3.

In every probability
We may yet discover

The whole country
Will not come back

From the sale of parent
And child. So far

As I can see, the loss
Is great and increasing.

I know they have desired
We should not know

What was for our own good,
But we cannot be all the cause

Of all that has been done.

4.

We wish to act. We may yet.
But we have to learn what their

Character and moral conduct
Will present. We have it in

Contemplation to wait and see.
If good, we shall be glad; if

Evil, then we must meet evil
As best we can.

5.

Father, mother, son, daughter, man.
And if that family is sold:
                    Please—

We cannot—
            Please—
                    We have got to—

Please—
            The children—
Mother and Father and husband and—

All of you—
            All—
                    I have no more—

How soon and unexpectedly cut off
Many, many, very many times.

from *The Believer*

Harm's Way

◇ ◇ ◇

It sounds like a country road.
It sounds like the swerve
Into the oncoming lane
Of a blind curve,
One teenager goading another
About their nerve;

It sounds like a wet stretch
Where a bridge tosses
Its back over a river
And a valley of mosses,
The humble guardrail studded
With makeshift crosses,

Like the shrug of black ice
As the cold gets colder
Running next to the ditch
Off the soft shoulder
Where the odometer stops
And no one gets older,

Or the path in a fairy tale
Through an ancient wood
Where the crumbs you dropped are gobbled
And you're lost for good.
And I would keep you out of it
If I only could.

from *The Hopkins Review*

ARTHUR SZE

The White Orchard

◇   ◇   ◇

Under a supermoon, you gaze into the orchard—

a glass blower shapes a glowing orange mass into a horse—

you step into a space where you once lived—

crushed mica glitters on plastered walls—

a raccoon strolls in moonlight along the top of an adobe wall—

swimming in a pond, we notice a reflected cottonwood on the water—

clang: a deer leaps over the gate—

every fifteen minutes an elephant is shot for its tusks—

you mark a bleached earless lizard against the snowfall of this white page—

the skins of eggplants glistening in a garden—

our bodies glistening by firelight—

though skunks once ravaged corn, our bright moments cannot be ravaged—

sleeping near a canal, you hear lapping waves—

at dawn, waves lapping and the noise of men unloading scallops and shrimp—

no noise of gunshots—

you focus on the branches of hundred-year-old apple trees—

opening the door, we find red and yellow rose petals scattered on our bed—

then light years—

you see pear branches farther in the orchard as the moon rises—

branches bending under the snow of this white page—

from *The Kenyon Review*

Duty

◇ ◇ ◇

When he tells the story now
he's at the center of it,

everyone else in the house
falling into the backdrop—

my mother, grandmother,
an uncle, all dead now—props

in our story: father and daughter
caught in memory's half-light.

I'm too young to recall it,
so his story becomes *the* story:

1969, Hurricane Camille
bearing down, the old house

shuddering as if it will collapse.
Rain pours into every room

and he has to keep moving,
keep me out of harm's way—

a father's first duty: to protect.
And so, in the story, he does:

I am small in his arms, perhaps
even sleeping. Water is rising

around us and there is no
higher place he can take me

than this, memory forged
in the storm's eye: a girl

clinging to her father. What
can I do but this? Let him

tell it again and again as if
it's always been only us,

and that, when it mattered,
he was the one who saved me.

from *Time*

OCEAN VUONG

Partly True Poem
Reflected in a Mirror

◊   ◊   ◊

*i want to find a gun / and change myself / he said / in the dream only a
week before his mother called / no hello only / her breath a windmill
crashing slowly into my head / this face already changed since heavy
rain left november too bloody / to read in a boy finds a bridge and
becomes / everywhere and i decide against / tuesday / vandross on the
stereo muted tv / the room pink / with images of a bloody dictator / my
face the shade of strawberry icing / as i sit through one war / another
hold / the page closer to the glass dammit / imagine yourself in / real
life / there should be tears / there should be / a reason but all i have /
is the voice: *17 children are gunned down in afghanistan today* / and i think:
shouldn't it be *gunned up?* / doesn't the bullet / in a child / become an
angel-seed / the beginning / of "heaven" / *how dare you* / i mutter to
myself / and the face / is only a little "prettier" than yesterday / which
is enough / so i step into the n train doors opening / the linebreak i
finished / schuyler's book / his grip still warm on my shoulder / words
all blurry / the last time / someone borrowed him was may 13 1981 /
which makes me sadder / than mondays in the library / reading all the
heroes who killed themselves / trying to save / my life / but the pills
were like / "the teeth of an angel" i said / into the mirror / said i'd make
it / to 34th st. but now i'm not sure / what i smoked is working / i take
long hits / cause i don't have healthcare / a line here / and there keeps
my hands from shaking / barely made it to brooklyn college / without
palms wet again / clutching the seats i'm sick / and sorry / for the scar
on your face even / at night the day brighter / as a memory / the young
poet with a mustache / sitting in the dusty classroom says / *don't worry
you have an edge / your friend died plus / you're asian* and i want / to take his*

hand and lie down in the room / lit only with broken glass / a coffee table axed to pieces / the statue of a plastic buddha / decapitated / and there no more prayers / at the prow of you / instead / i said *have you ever been fucked in the ass? . . . no / no i don't mean figuratively* / you see / all this trouble / just to make some sense / just to make a ghost appear / on paper / so you can see me in this mirror and maybe it's 8pm there / after all / this face already gone / maybe this is just to say / that i found the gun / and changed / the world instead / and now it's just you and me / dear reader / meeting each other for / the first time in a room dark / as the insides of / our skulls / and look i'm sorry i'm reflecting / the two gashes in your face / i would stitch them up / but you'll never see again

from *Freeman's*

Still Life: Stevens's Wallet on a Key West Hotel Dresser

◇   ◇   ◇

Its alligator skin, now pliant from the years
    of summoning & concealing, of the jaw
        snapping open & shut, adding & subtracting

the large old-fangled twenties, immaculately crisp,
    venereally green & a cache of Jeffersons
        for setting down at the betting booth in Hialeah.

Chaste Diana's greyhounds: how agilely
    they bolt & quicken, rounding the palm-lined
        backstretch as their metal rabbit quarry

taunts them ever faster. Sometimes a payoff,
    sometimes not. Sometimes torts,
        sometimes the palacios of Crispin or Hoon.

The wallet hide is wafer thin. He could count,
    were he so inclined, the various archipelagos
        which map the folds, stained a tasteful oxblood.

Thus money is a kind of poetry, though to be so
    its binding must be flawless, Francophilic,
        like a leather-bound Laforgue or Mallarmé,

pages rustling *en plein air*, a garden perhaps,
    a girl in a straw hat, mouthing some pages aloud.
        & now, a close-up of the contents: Kodak

of Elsie, her new stove a-gleam. Holly riding
    upon his shoulders against a backdrop
        of Connecticut snow. Calling cards with logo

of the Hartford Indemnity—the imperious stag.
    & beyond all this, the iambs to mold
        the Golem of the Major Man. Melodies

of trumps & zithers, of variegate colors
    unknown in nature. O Imagination—
        stupefyingly Grand. But the heart,

the heart is human, vexed & brittle. The heart
    will not suffice. O the twenties & the tens,
        & the lowly Jeffersons. & the tie clasp, the lapis

cufflinks. Seltzer dispenser & a decent scotch,
    The Miami Herald, dated 29 July, 1932. The Bonus Army's
        Hooverville in sepia rubble. The roiling Potomac,

an equestrian General George S. Patton, his terrible
    swift sword raised up above the dead & gassed.
        In the distance, the reflecting pool, the obelisk

& Memorials. But here, in the oval glass, two soft hands
    administer pomade, a tortoiseshell comb has fashioned
        an exacting part, dabs of cologne beneath

each ear. Time for highballs as the sun begins
    its regal plummet, & the twilit palms
        commence their susurrant adagios.

from *AGNI*

KEVIN YOUNG

Hive

◊　◊　◊

The honey bees' exile
    is almost complete.
You can carry

them from hive
    to hive, the child thought
& that is what

he tried, walking
    with them thronging
between his pressed palms.

Let him be right.
    Let the gods look away
as always. Let this boy

who carries the entire
    actual, whirring
world in his calm

unwashed hands,
    barely walking, bear
us all there

buzzing, unstung.

from Poem-a-Day

CONTRIBUTORS' NOTES AND COMMENTS

DILRUBA AHMED was born in Philadelphia, Pennsylvania, in 1973. Her book, *Dhaka Dust* (Graywolf Press, 2011), won the Bakeless Prize. A graduate of Warren Wilson College's MFA Program for Writers, she has taught at Bryn Mawr College and in Chatham University's low-residency MFA program.

Of "Phase One," Ahmed writes: "After #45 was voted into office, I found myself grappling daily with a mix of very strong feelings: resentment, anger, what felt like hatred. Worse, my bitterness was not directed strictly toward some abstract or nameless entity, but also toward some individual people in my life. I knew I'd be unable to function with such terrible feelings, and yet I struggled to find a way beyond them. What kind of mind-set, I wondered, could grant one the perspective that transcends resentment and anger, and inches toward understanding, or even healing? A parental view, one of unconditional love? An effort to approach a godlike sense of distance, so far removed it might enable one to observe with what I imagined to be a mix of big-hearted forgiveness, maybe pity, or gentle reproach? Or simply detachment? Nothing I could envision felt authentic or even feasible to me.

"I found myself pondering what it takes to be truly empathetic, to have genuine compassion, to open oneself to understanding even under seemingly impossible circumstances. I grew interested in the notion of forgiveness, with self-forgiveness as a precursor to that. The idea of turning inward, as some kind of initial step, felt both genuine and viable. The notion that the understanding or forgiveness that we might extend to others must begin within began to resonate with me.

"While I've tried to funnel my strong feelings into action via local political movements, I don't know that I've found effective ways to cope with my anger and bitterness, or whether healing and forgiveness are possible—or even warranted—in some scenarios. In the meantime, this poem happened. I owe a debt to Ross White for providing critical feed-back on early versions of 'Phase One.' The 'white curtain' in the poem refers to 'Try to Praise the Mutilated World' by Adam Zagajewski."

ROSA ALCALÁ was born in Paterson, New Jersey, in 1969, to Spanish immigrants. She is the author of three books of poetry, most recently *MyOTHER TONGUE* (Futurepoem, 2017). As a translator she has focused on contemporary Latin American women poets living in the United States. She edited and cotranslated *The New and Selected Poems of Cecilia Vicuña* (Kelsey Street Press, 2018). She has received an NEA Literature Translation Fellowship and is a professor of creative writing in the University of Texas at El Paso's Bilingual MFA Program, where she has taught since 2004.

Alcalá writes: " 'You & the Raw Bullets' is part of a series in the second person that began as a way to speak to versions of who I had been as a younger woman. The poem began while I listened to some-one on the radio talk about the importance of referring to the perpetra-tors of sexual harassment and assault, not just the victims—that sexual assault was actively committed, not just passively received. Thinking through this while the radio report played, I had a vision of a bullet, or bullets, which I called 'raw,' entering my mouth over and over again. These bullets were the many times my younger body had to accept and swallow subtle or outright violations and feelings of fear in pub-lic spaces: the grope on public transportation, the catcall on the street, a physical assault in a park. And all the bullets I'd swallowed over the course of my life were still lodged in my older body. This realiza-tion made me angry, not just for myself, but for all the others whose bodies—some of them targets for real bullets—must navigate daily all types of dangers normalized by a racist and patriarchal culture. It made me angry for my daughter, whom I had brought into this toxic world. The poem began to transform these feelings of personal desperation into something powerful: the recognition that my body in midlife was stronger than ever, and the possibility from there of collective action: What if we all took what we've swallowed and spit it back?"

MARGARET ATWOOD was born in Ottawa, Ontario, in 1939. Her latest book of short stories is *Stone Mattress: Nine Tales* (2014); her latest novel, *The Heart Goes Last* (2015). Of her many novels, *The Blind Assassin* won the Booker Prize in 2000; *Alias Grace* won the Giller Prize in Canada and the Premio Montello in Italy; and *The Handmaid's Tale* was adapted for the screen by Harold Pinter and became the basis of a critically acclaimed television series. *The Door* is her most recent volume of poetry (2007). Her most recent nonfiction books are *Payback: Debt and the Shadow Side of Wealth* (2008) and *In Other Worlds: SF and the Human Imagination* (2011). Atwood lives in Toronto with writer Graeme Gibson.

CATHERINE BARNETT was born in Washington, DC, in 1960. She is the author of three collections, *Human Hours* (winner of the 2018 *Believer* Book Award in Poetry and a *New York Times* "Best Poetry of 2018" selection), *The Game of Boxes* (James Laughlin Award of the Academy of American Poets), and *Into Perfect Spheres Such Holes Are Pierced.* She has won a Whiting Award and a Guggenheim Fellowship. She teaches in the creative writing program at NYU, is a Distinguished Lecturer at Hunter College, and lives in New York City, where she also works as an independent editor.

Of "Central Park," Barnett writes: "I see I carried both Elizabeth Bishop (with a slight variation to the opening of her marvelous 'Over 2,000 Illustrations and a Complete Concordance') and Emily Dickinson (with her radical negations) into Central Park, where the benches seem flush with praise and lament. When I found out how expensive the benches are, and how few remain, my old kleptomaniac tendencies were aroused, along with an echo of Eliot's (echoing Dante's) 'so many, / I had not thought death had undone so many.' I just saw the Bruce Nauman exhibition at MoMA and was moved by the way he subverts time and makes absence a presence (see his *Venice Fountains*). I love the way the benches in Central Park invite us to take the place of those who have disappeared, making our own inevitable disappearances all the more palpable and turning the benches into a common way station. Whether named for you or not, a bench is a humanizing form, allowing several people to sit together at the same time and take a rest of uncertain duration from clamor and uncertainty. In history, chairs were saved for the VIPs; benches were for all."

JOSHUA BENNETT was born in New York, New York, in 1988. He is the author of *The Sobbing School* (Penguin Books, 2016), which was a National Poetry Series winner, as well as *Being Property Once Myself: Blackness and the End of Man* (Harvard University Press, 2020), *Owed* (Penguin, 2020), and *Spoken Word: A Cultural History*, which is forthcoming from Knopf. In 2010, he delivered the commencement address at the University of Pennsylvania. He is an assistant professor of English and creative writing at Dartmouth College.

Bennett writes: "I wrote 'America Will Be' a little over a year ago, during a New York summer where my father and I would get breakfast at IHOP every other week. My father integrated his high school in Birmingham, Alabama, in 1966, and many of his most striking tales were about his time as a teenager in the Jim Crow South. He never made the experience sound all that heroic. Mostly, he described it as lonely, confusing. He talked about the difficulty of his schoolwork, and the forms of physical violence he had to navigate every day. He emphasized what it meant for him, as an individual human being, to spend his senior year in such an unforgiving, unfamiliar place; one that was, by design, meant to exclude him and the people he loved.

"The poem is my attempt to reflect this set of concerns, while also highlighting the astonishing fact of my father's courage, and persistence, in the midst of what might appear to be an altogether unlivable situation. The situation is always inextricably linked to what James Baldwin and others have called *the black condition*: our perpetual state of emergency and emergence. In that vein, this is a work of celebration, repair, and reclamation. It is my assertion that my father's irreducibly black America is a historical corrective, a present reality, and a vision for the future. It is a song for the myriad who are unheralded and nonetheless loved beyond measure."

FLEDA BROWN was born in Columbia, Missouri, in 1944. *The Woods Are on Fire*, her new and selected poems, was chosen by Ted Kooser for the University of Nebraska poetry series in 2017. She has nine previous collections of poems. Her work has twice appeared in *The Best American Poetry*. *Driving with Dvořák*, her memoir, was published in 2010 by the University of Nebraska Press. She is professor emerita at the University of Delaware, where she directed the Poets in the Schools program. She was poet laureate of Delaware from 2001 to 2007. She now lives with her husband, Jerry Beasley, in Traverse City, Michigan, and is on the faculty of the Rainier Writing Workshop, a low-residency MFA program in Tacoma, Washington.

Of "Afternoons at the Lake," Brown writes: "I'm not a game player, except under duress. I am so glad to have gotten a poem, at least, out of hours of suffering through Monopoly. Oh, that's not true. As often as I could, I've pawned off the chore on those who enjoyed it. It's the sheer greed, even in fun, that makes me twitchy. The game's orchestrated stages of wealth-gaining, with its nasty side effects. Midas with his literally hardened heart. And that iconic rich guy in the top hat, the God of the whole thing, who wins past wanting to win. The best antidote to that I know is Keats. Is poetry. Is standing on the end of the dock where there are no goals except remembering the lines of the poem."

SUMITA CHAKRABORTY was born in Nyack, New York, in 1987 and raised in Massachusetts. She has received a Ruth Lilly and Dorothy Sargent Rosenberg prize from the Poetry Foundation. She teaches at Emory University in Atlanta, Georgia. "Essay on Joy" is from her first poetry collection, *Arrow*, which is forthcoming from Alice James Books in the United States and Carcanet Press in the United Kingdom in September 2020.

Of "Essay on Joy," Chakraborty writes: "This poem is about the afterlives of acts that occur at the intersections of emotional and physical violence, especially in the context of domestic violence, especially during childhood. I wanted to think about the simultaneously ritualized and unpredictable nature of this kind of violence—which is why I hope the poem reads both as a cohesive and circular myth and as though its loops of thought sometimes jump with a verse-paragraph break into a strange new space—and I wanted to think about what kinds of affect scripts we write in the aftermath of such violence, for which I draw on autobiography and on Spinoza's *Ethics*. Along the way the poem is invested in thinking through the relationship between embodied self-perception, physical exertion, appetites (for eros, for food, for danger, for pain), and labor. *What kinds of bodily encounters follow a body's encounter with these forms of violence?* That's one of the poem's largest questions.

"The story of a large number of dead grackles falling from the sky in Boston—which is where I spent most of my life (although I didn't live there when this happened)—is true, and remains unexplained. It is true, too, that one of their toes points backward."

VICTORIA CHANG was born in Detroit, Michigan, in 1970. Her new book of poems, *OBIT*, will be published by Copper Canyon Press in 2020. *Barbie Chang* was published by Copper Canyon in 2017. *The Boss* (McSweeney's, 2013) won a PEN Center USA Literary Award and a California Book Award. Other poetry books are *Salvinia Molesta* and *Circle*. Her children's picture book, *Is Mommy?*, was illustrated by Marla Frazee and published by Beach Lane Books/Simon & Schuster in 2015 and was named a *New York Times* Notable Book. She has received a Guggenheim Fellowship and the Poetry Society of America's Alice Fay Di Castagnola Award. She lives in Los Angeles and teaches in Antioch's low-residency MFA program.

Of "Six Obits," Chang writes: "After my mom died in 2015 following a long illness (pulmonary fibrosis), I absolutely did not want to write about it or write elegies. One day on the radio, I learned about a documentary film called *Obit* about writers of obituaries. That word with the long O and the hard T rung and touched me. I sat at a stoplight thinking about how when someone dies, everything dies. I went home and over two weeks and in a state of frenzy (and deep sadness), wrote seventy-five of these *OBIT* poems. I meant their formal shape to resemble newspaper obits. The form helped both to constrain my sadness and expound upon it in new ways."

CHEN CHEN was born in Xiamen, China, in 1989. He is the author of *When I Grow Up I Want to Be a List of Further Possibilities*, which won the 2018 Thom Gunn Award for Gay Poetry. He teaches at Brandeis University.

Of "I Invite My Parents to a Dinner Party," Chen writes: "I wrote this poem after a conversation with Muriel Leung in which she asked what would happen if I imagined my parents having to make a bridge to me, instead of the other way around. For so long I've had to be the one reaching out to them, doing that draining work of educating them out of their homophobia. Also, I've realized how frustrated I am with movies and TV shows that depict the coming-out process as a onetime event, either immediately triumphant or tragic. I think usually the process is recursive, messy, the pains as well as the joys stranger than one might anticipate."

LEONARD COHEN (1934–2016) was a Companion of the Order of Canada, the nation's highest civilian honor. The Jewish-Canadian singer, songwriter, poet, novelist, and painter was born in the Westmount area of Montreal. Brought up as an orthodox Jew, he was educated at McGill University, where he studied with Irving Layton and Louis Dudek. A member of the "Montreal School of Poets," he published his first book of poems, *Let Us Compare Mythologies*, at the age of twenty-two. In 1967, Cohen moved to the United States to pursue a recording career. He wrote "Hallelujah," "Suzanne," "Chelsea Hotel," "Bird on a Wire," and "I'm Your Man." Cohen continued to observe the Sabbath even when on tour and performed for Israeli troops during the Yom Kippur War in 1973. In a 2016 interview with *The New Yorker*, Bob Dylan said that Cohen's "gift of genius is his connection to the music of the spheres." Cohen's thirteen books of poems include *Flowers for Hitler*, *Book of Mercy*, and *Book of Longing*. He wrote two novels, *The Favorite Game* and *Beautiful Losers*. "People are doing their courting, people are finding their wives, people are making babies, people are washing their dishes, people are getting through the day, with songs that we may find insignificant," he observed. "But their significance is affirmed by others. There's always someone affirming the significance of a song by taking a woman into his arms or by getting through the night. That's what dignifies the song. Songs don't dignify human activity. Human activity dignifies the song."

Laura Cronk was born in New Castle, Indiana, in 1977. She is the author of *Having Been an Accomplice* from Persea Books and teaches at the New School in New York. Her second book of poems is forthcoming from Persea in 2020.

Of "Like a Cat," Cronk writes: "This poem emerged during a period when I was trying to write a poem a day in the spirit of David Lehman's *The Daily Mirror*. Writing every day, when I manage it, makes space to take passing thoughts seriously. During this time my family was in the midst of deciding to get a dog. This poem let me access the sadness I still had about not being able to have a cat. It was a bargain I made when I married my husband. His cat allergies are no joke. But his many catlike qualities came rushing toward me as I wrote. He's even a Scorpio, like all true cats."

Kate Daniels, born in Richmond, Virginia, in 1953, is director of creative writing at Vanderbilt University. She also teaches writing at the Washington Baltimore Center for Psychoanalysis. Her sixth collection of poetry, *In the Months of My Son's Recovery*, was published earlier this year.

Of "Metaphor-less," Daniels writes: "I have brought my poetry into healthcare settings for twenty-five years as poet-in-residence at Duke and Vanderbilt Medical Centers and as a writing teacher at the Washington Baltimore Center for Psychoanalysis. Nevertheless, nothing prepared me for the violent shock of discovering, in 2012, that a member of my family had been drawn into the national opioid epidemic. Since then, I have written many poems emerging from the experience. They are collected in two volumes: *Three Syllables Describing Addiction* and *In the Months of My Son's Recovery*. I also conduct workshops, called "Writing for Recovery," aimed at people whose lives have been affected by other people's addictions. Like all the poems I have written on this subject, 'Metaphor-less' concerns itself with the collateral human damage of addiction (the 'Family Illness'), and does not try to represent the experience of Substance Use Disorder, or those afflicted by it. For more information, see my website at www.katedanielspoetry andprose.com."

CARL DENNIS was born in St. Louis, Missouri, in 1939. His most recent book of poems, *Night School*, was published by Penguin Books in 2018. A winner of the Pulitzer Prize and the Ruth Lilly Poetry Prize, he taught for many years in the English department of the State University of New York, and in the Warren Wilson writing program in North Carolina. He lives in Buffalo, New York.

Dennis writes: " 'Armed Neighbor' is presented as an effort to reason with someone whom the speaker is not likely to address directly, working on the magical faith that an imaginary conversation may with luck become a real one."

TOI DERRICOTTE was born in Hamtramck, Michigan, in 1941. Her sixth poetry collection, *I: New and Selected Poems*, was published in 2019 by the University of Pittsburgh Press. With poet Cornelius Eady, she cofounded the Cave Canem Foundation in 1996. This much-honored poet is professor emerita at the University of Pittsburgh and a former chancellor of the Academy of American Poets.

Derricotte writes: " 'An apology to the reader' is another kind of argument with silence."

THOMAS DEVANEY was born in Philadelphia, Pennsylvania, in 1969. His new book is *You Are the Battery* (Black Square Editions, 2019). He is a 2014 Pew Fellow. His new and selected *Getting to Philadelphia* is forthcoming from Hanging Loose Press. He is the author of five previous collections of poetry, including *Runaway Goat Cart* (Hanging Loose) and *The Picture that Remains* with the photographer Will Brown (The Print Center). He lives in Philadelphia and teaches at Haverford College.

Devaney writes: "My poem 'Brilliant Corners' is a map of a life fortified by music. From my early teens to my late twenties I was a musician and started off college as a music major. The poem is dedicated to the visual artist Jennie C. Jones. At parties Jones and I often wind up in a corner somewhere talking up a storm about our appetites for sound. It dawned on me that Thelonious Monk's *Brilliant Corners* is an apt description of some of Jennie's work. Now I realize that in those passionate, hilarious, extended conversations, Jennie and I were both swapping notes about our own sonic lodestars."

NATALIE DIAZ was born and raised in the Fort Mojave Indian Village in Needles, California, on the banks of the Colorado River.

Diaz writes: "In 'Skin-Light,' I was thinking about a ball game that was played throughout the Americas, in several different forms, part ceremony, part social. It was similar to what we now might call basketball and even futbol or soccer. My knowings and inquiries of my body have been shaped by my experience of the game of basketball. I have a freedom from and tethering to the body that carry over into the way I do and feel most things, including touch and tenderness. This poem is an inquiry, a wonder about what it means that violence and pain exist in simultaneity with joy and the ecstatic. And is submission to desire victory or defeat? What does it mean that I have been made, both in a game and in love, by these relationships? And what if the answer to all of these is 'light,' which is the beginning of a question?"

JOANNE DOMINIQUE DWYER was born in Rockaway Beach, Queens, New York. She currently resides in Northern New Mexico. Her book of poems is *Belle Laide* by Sarabande Books, 2013. She has received a Rona Jaffe Award and holds an MFA from Warren Wilson's program for writers. She cites her time spent in her local community with elderly and teens, through the Alzheimer's Poetry Project and the Witter Bynner Foundation, respectively, as her most profound experience of poetry as a means of metamorphosis and transcendence.

Dwyer writes: "When revisiting my poem 'Decline in the Adoration of Jack-in-the-Pulpits' in order to provide commentary, I became aware of the hefty sorrow in the poem that I was not so acutely aware of while creating it. The impetus for the poem—a small plant, which resembles a sermonizing man—transmigrated into a commentary on the deficit of appreciation for nature and for the simpler things and ways of life, in stark comparison to contemporary aberrant focus on self-infatuation and electronic devices. Revisiting the poem was a bit like caliginous water rising up from a sealed and derelict basement to a sunlit widow's peak lookout. A more dexterous perception of my deep-cut heartbreak around that cultural obsession that orients away from reverence of the natural world engulfed me and continues to do so.

"It has since occurred to me that during the process of fabricating our poems, of conjuring, galvanizing, and animating images, free associating and riding the wave of instinct, of adjuring forth our lines, words, syllables, and sounds, at times as if we are blindfolded and trying to pin the tail on the donkey or randomly selecting Bingo coordinates from a bowl, we are in a bubble of protection, in a velvet or silk cloth of separation from emotive content or rhetorical agenda. Despite dark content, we sail a bit in a bath of mood-elevating neurotransmitters that are the byproduct of engaging and minding the stove of imagination.

"For me, imagination reigns sublime; is as sacred as love.

"My gratitude to Major Jackson.

"And to Tony Hoagland, who, because of his wildly generous spirit, would have celebrated my poem landing in this volume. And then he would have also reminded me of the fleeting, fragile, and impermanent nature of everything."

MARTÍN ESPADA was born in Brooklyn, New York, in 1957. His latest collection of poems from Norton is called *Vivas to Those Who Have Failed* (W. W. Norton, 2016). Other books of poems include *The Trouble Ball* (Norton, 2011), *The Republic of Poetry* (Norton, 2006), and *Alabanza* (Norton, 2003). His book of essays, *Zapata's Disciple* (1998), was banned in Tucson as part of the Mexican-American Studies Program outlawed by the state of Arizona. A former tenant lawyer in Greater Boston's Latino community, Espada is a professor of English at the University of Massachusetts-Amherst.

Of "I Now Pronounce You Dead," Espada writes: "The poem focuses on a historic injustice that still resonates: the execution of

Nicola Sacco and Bartolomeo Vanzetti. Many of the details come from an account of the execution in the August 23, 1927, edition of *The New York Times*. The poem draws a connection between the repression of immigrants past and present, as well as the ultimate futility of that repression. The former site of Charlestown State Prison, where Sacco and Vanzetti were executed, is the current site of Bunker Hill Community College—a school with a large immigrant population, speaking in many tongues. As the saying goes: *Aquí estamos y no nos vamos.* Here we are and here we stay. (I have visited and read at the college multiple times.) The poem is also about the paradox of a good man in a bad system—Warden William Hendry, 'almost overcome by the execution' according to the *Times*—and the compromise with lethal injustice that would haunt him."

NAUSHEEN EUSUF is a PhD candidate in English at Boston University. She is the author of *Not Elegy, But Eros* (2017), published simultaneously by NYQ Books in the United States and Bengal Lights Books in Bangladesh. A native of Bangladesh, she was born in its capital, Dhaka, in 1980.

Eusuf writes: " 'The Analytic Hour' is about psychoanalytic therapy as an experience of estrangement and alienation, rather than connection. Even with a well-meaning therapist, the experience can be profoundly disorienting—a loss of self, a mortification of the self. Therapy has the potential to harm as well as to heal: like Plato's *pharmakon*, the poison and the cure are the same."

VIEVEE FRANCIS is the author of three books of poetry: *Blue-Tail Fly* (Wayne State University Press, 2006), *Horse in the Dark* (Northwestern University Press, 2016), and *Forest Primeval*, which won the 2017 Kingsley Tufts Poetry Award. Her work has appeared in three previous volumes of *The Best American Poetry* (*2010, 2014,* and *2017*). She teaches poetry writing in the Callaloo Creative Writing Workshop (United States, United Kingdom, and Barbados). In 2009 she received a Rona Jaffe Writer's Award, and in 2010, a Kresge Fellowship. She is an associate editor of *Callaloo* and teaches at Dartmouth College.

GABRIELA GARCIA was born in New York City in 1984 to immigrant parents from Cuba and Mexico. She has received a Rona Jaffe Foundation Writer's Award. She received an MFA in fiction from Purdue

University. *Of Women and Salt*, a novel, is forthcoming from Ecco/
HarperCollins. Connect with her at www.gabrielagarciawriter.com.

Garcia writes: " 'Guantanamera' is the title of a famous Cuban song
and poem that my mother would sometimes sing to me when I was a
child: 'I am a sincere person from the land where the palm grows / and
before I die I want to cast these words from my soul . . . / with the poor
of the Earth I want to share my lot.' The nineteenth-century Cuban
independence fighter and poet Jose Martí penned the original verses,
which eventually became a song covered by dozens of artists from Joan
Baez to Wyclef Jean. 'Guantanamera' also became one of salsa queen
Celia Cruz's best-known numbers. I've danced to 'Guantanamera'
at parties in Miami, heard it played on melancholy guitars along the
malecón in Habana, and read its words etched onto the marble busts
of freedom fighters on both sides of the ocean. I wanted to capture the
cadence and rhythm of this song so etched into my own history, and
pay tribute to the larger forces that shaped it—the poets, the fighters,
the artists, the complex issues of race and class and politics and migra-
tion that have shaped its lyrics and music. I wanted to pay tribute to the
complicated history that led to me, a child sitting at a kitchen table in
Miami, listening to my displaced mother hum a tune to dissolve the
years and miles weighing heavy on her. I was also thinking about the
resilience of my parents, of all immigrants, of their children: that there
is no ocean deep enough—or wall high enough—to break our spirit."

AMY GERSTLER was born in San Diego, California, in 1956. Her books
of poems include *Scattered at Sea* (Penguin Books, 2015) and *Dearest
Creature* (Penguin, 2009), which was named a *New York Times Book
Review* Notable Book. Her previous twelve books include *Ghost Girl*,
Crown of Weeds, *Nerve Storm*, and *Bitter Angel*, which won the National
Book Critics Circle Award in poetry. She received a Guggenheim Fel-
lowship in 2018. In 2019 she received the C.D. Wright Award from
the Foundation for Contemporary Arts. She was the guest editor of
The Best American Poetry 2010.

Of "Update," Gerstler writes: "An unsent letter to the dead is how I
mostly think of this poem. The state of lost-ness and confusion I tum-
bled into after my mother's death, which re-seizes me from time to
time no matter how many years have passed since her demise, domi-
nates this elegy for me. I have long depended upon the power of poems
to speak to and about the dead, to construct a bridge, however imag-

inary or aspirational, between the dead and the living. This poem I think attempts to make that connection in a moment when the speaker is feeling particularly unmoored and bereft, and looks to surrounding household objects and aspects of nature to reflect and amplify her longing for someone long gone. The poem is also inflected with dejection about the results of the 2016 American presidential election, about which the speaker 'updates' the dead loved one in a euphemistic sort of way, as the speaker vainly begs for comfort, or some hint about what's to come. At least that's my read. What's yours?"

CAMILLE GUTHRIE was born in Seattle in 1971. Her books of poetry include *Articulated Lair: Poems for Louise Bourgeois* (Subpress, 2013). *Diamonds*, her new book, will appear from BOA Editions in fall 2021. She lives in Vermont, where she is the director of undergraduate writing initiatives at Bennington College.

Of "Virgil, Hey," Guthrie writes: "The urgency of school mornings induces hyperbole. A tribute to my mom friends, who know well the hell it is to get your kids ready for school in the morning, this poem alludes to Canto I of Dante's *Inferno* in the Longfellow translation: 'Midway upon the journey of our life / I found myself within a forest dark, / For the straightforward pathway had been lost. // Ah me! how hard a thing it is to say.' Surely Dante speaks for us middle-aged parents whom love has separated us from our reason. I also allude to a poem by T'ao Ch'ien (or T'ao Yüan-ming) called 'Scolding My Sons,' translated by David Hinton, which begins: 'My temples covered all in white, I'm / slack-muscled and loose-skinned for good // now.'"

YONA HARVEY was born in Cincinnati, Ohio, in 1974. She is the author of two poetry collections: *Hemming the Water* (2013), winner of the Kate Tufts Discovery Award, and the forthcoming *You Don't Have to Go to Mars for Love* (2020), both from Four Way Books. She contributed to Marvel's *World of Wakanda* (2016) and is coauthor with Ta-Nehisi Coates of Marvel's *Black Panther and The Crew* (2017).

Of "Dark and Lovely After Take-Off (A Future)," Harvey writes: "I used to judge harshly two women. I called them 'The Women from Mars.' It didn't take long, though, before I realized I was one of them. When I was revising this poem, I was also finalizing a piece for the visual artist Alisha Wormsley. Alisha's art views black women through the lens of what she calls the Fifth Dimension: the past, present, and future coexist alongside one another. This poem honors that holistic existence and values its own preoccupations and tangents. One more thing: when I'm overwhelmed by too many ideas and emotions, I sometimes use formal (or informal) parameters—in this case, syllabics. I'm indebted to the joyful artistry of both Alisha and the poet Ross Gay, who gave me the courage to let this poem go."

ROBERT HASS was born in San Francisco in 1941. He teaches literature at the University of California at Berkeley. A book of his poems, *Summer Snow*, is forthcoming from Ecco Press. He was guest editor of *The Best American Poetry 2001*.

Of "Dancing," Hass writes: "For the account of the history of the Kalashnikov, I am indebted to the work of C. J. Chivers in *The New York Times*, February 15, 2018. The description of Robert La Salle's entry into the Great Lakes is to be found in Francis Parkman's *La Salle and the Discovery of the Great West* (1869). There have been so many mass murders in the United States in the two decades since fifteen children were killed in a school in Colorado in 1999 that it is probably necessary to remind readers of the occasion that elicited this poem. It was the murder of forty-nine people in a nightclub in Orlando, Florida, on June 12, 2016."

TERRANCE HAYES was born in Columbia, South Carolina, in 1971. His most recent publications include *American Sonnets for My Past and Future Assassin* (Penguin Books, 2018) and *To Float in the Space Between: A Life and Work in Conversation with the Life and Work of Etheridge Knight* (Wave Books, 2018). He was guest editor of *The Best American Poetry 2014*.

Of "American Sonnet for My Past and Future Assassin," Hayes writes: "I mostly just want to recommend the poems of LeRoi Jones to fellow poetry lovers. You may be familiar with the title poem of his 1961 debut, *Preface to a Twenty Volume Suicide Note*, but I'm telling you those other poems are fire, too. Near the end of the poem he writes:

> And then last night, I tiptoed up
> To my daughter's room and heard her
> Talking to someone, and when I opened
> The door, there was no one there . . .

It's almost as if he hears his daughter talking to a premonition, a phantom of his future self. . . . The second and final poetry collection of LeRoi Jones, 1964's *The Dead Lecturer*, is also tremendous. In 'Footnote to a Pretentious Book' when Jones writes, 'A long life, to you. My friend. I / tell that to myself, slowly, sucking / my lip,' it's almost as if he is speaking to the Baraka he will become following the assassination of Malcolm X a year later. 'Footnote to a Pretentious Book' is a phenomenal poem. LeRoi Jones? Amiri Baraka? Poetry lovers, you do not have to choose between them."

JUAN FELIPE HERRERA was born in Fowler, California, in the Central Valley of San Joaquín, in 1948. He has served as poet laureate of California (2012–2015) and United States Poet Laureate (2015–2017). His most recent collection of poems is *Notes on the Assemblage* (City Lights, 2015).

Herrera writes: " 'Roll Under the Waves' is an attempt to cut into the existential layers of our migrant experience, an illegalized life, these days—that of running, escape, being chased by patrols, feverish, for an illusory openness to a land we once called home. Under extreme odds, as always. The border-crossing trail is ever-present danger, suffering, the last seconds of survival. I am interested in drawing out the inscapes of women, men, and children pulled down into such torturous depths. What happened to kindness?"

EDWARD HIRSCH was born in Chicago in 1950 and educated at Grinnell College and the University of Pennsylvania. He has published nine books of poems, including *The Living Fire: New and Selected Poems* and *Gabriel: A Poem*, a book-length elegy for his son. "Stranger by Night" is the title poem of his tenth collection, which will be published by Knopf in 2020. He has published five prose books, among them *Poet's Choice* and *A Poet's Glossary*, a compendium of poetic terms. He was the guest editor of *The Best American Poetry 2016*. He is a MacArthur Fellow and serves as president of the John Simon Guggenheim Memorial Foundation.

Of "Stranger by Night," Hirsch writes: "A. R. Ammons said that 'a poem is a walk.' My short-lined one-sentence poem is a daily urban walk that has suddenly become more hesitant, difficult, and precarious. I wanted to treat my eye disease with matter-of-fact exactitude and enact how it has estranged my relationship to the world after dark, a world that has grown deeper and more mysterious by night. My friends have been dying at an alarming rate, and I wrote this poem at a time when I kept getting sideswiped by memories."

Jane Hirshfield, born in New York City in 1953, is the author of eight poetry books, including *The Beauty* and *Come, Thief.* She has also written two books of essays, *Nine Gates* and *Ten Windows*, and is editor or cotranslator of four books presenting the work of world poets from the past. A chancellor emerita of The Academy of American Poets, she has won fellowships from the Guggenheim and Rockefeller foundations. "Ledger" is the title poem of her forthcoming book, to be published by Knopf in 2020.

Hirshfield writes: "I wrote 'Ledger' in 2016, on Captiva Island in Florida, while working at the late painter Robert Rauschenberg's former studio and home, now an artists' retreat. That January–February was the wettest in Florida records, and Captiva, as the poem indicates, is five feet above sea level at its highest point. I had already been writing poems about climate change and the environmental crisis. Wading each day to my studio calf-deep in the reality of sea-rise magnified both urgency-awareness and the sharpness of grief. Midway through my time there, the Army Corps of Engineers released into the Caloosahatchee River the rising waters from Florida's central Lake Okeechobee. A plume of algae toxic from agricultural runoff poured into the Gulf. For the rest of my stay, dead fish washed up on the beaches.

"Climate-change science consists largely of numerical accounting. In both rising and falling numbers, we track the damage already done and predict the biosphere's future. 'Ledger,' then, is a poem of both precise noting and mourning. Its repetitions of sound are the metronome ticking of loss. The "million fired-clay bones" allude to a project (http://www.onemillionbones.net/the-project/) one of my fellow artists-in-residence had helped create: the bones, handmade by many different communities, were laid out in 2013 on the National Mall in Washington, DC, to make visible the world's mounting toll of war-atrocity and genocide. The poem's ancient Chinese measurement of distance (*li*), its Russian music and poetry, Polish potatoes, and elk heads on the wall of a U.S. bar, are equally meant to acknowledge and make visible the measures of our shared fates. Ecological catastrophe crosses time, border, species, and boundary. What happens to any of us happens to us all.

"The account books of art and of science are inseparable and mutually needed. Each brings a way to take in realities hard to see without assistance; each helps us ponder—individually and together—how to live in this paradise-beauty we have been given, ours to pass on or destroy."

JAMES HOCH was born in Camden, New Jersey, in 1967. He lives in the Hudson Valley and is a professor of creative writing at Ramapo College of New Jersey and a visiting faculty member at Sarah Lawrence College.

Of "Sunflowers," Hoch writes: "I like to drag my sons to museums. They usually go reluctantly. But, after a period of adjustment, they settle in nicely with a piece. Hardly ever am I right about which piece will draw their eye. When they are ready to leave, they are really ready to leave.

"Intimacy, proximity and exchange, is something I think about often. It's a complicated space. I suppose this poem is a way of engaging some of the difficulties that come from intimacy. Uncertainty and vulnerability chief among them.

"How do I say to my child the facts of war? How do I not minimize nor glorify war, especially when the war is so proximate to your life? Sometimes exposition is blunt force trauma. Sometimes it unclouds.

"After the attacks of September 11, 2001, my brother signed up for the special forces and was deployed to Afghanistan in 2003. I stayed home and wrote poems.

"The war is still going on, though not so many Americans are paying attention, and sometimes I, too, forget it wages. Then, I will be doing something, like looking at a painting, or talking to my son, and it will find its way in. Once anything is inside you, you can't help but feel complicit."

BOB HOLMAN founded the Bowery Poetry Club in New York City. A Columbia graduate, Bob ran inventive poetry slams at the Nuyorican Poets Café and other venues. He has two new books coming out—*Life Poem*, a book-length poem he wrote when he was twenty, and a new and selected volume, *The Unspoken*, both from YBK/Bowery Books. He has taught at Princeton, Columbia, NYU, Bard College, and The New School and is cofounder of the Endangered Language Alliance. www.bobholman.com

Holman writes: " 'All Praise Cecil Taylor' first appeared in Quincy Troupe's NYU literary magazine, *Black Renaissance Noire*, and was performed at the Poetry Project's New Year's Marathon, 2019. I take this poet job seriously, learned the griot part from Papa Susso, who taught me all about Praise Poems. Poems are made of words, they make memories real, and they become music. Cecil told me that. Now you know."

GARRETT HONGO was born in Volcano, Hawai'i, and grew up in Los Angeles. His work includes *Coral Road: Poems*, *Volcano: A Memoir of Hawai'i*, and *The Mirror Diary: Selected Essays*. He has received a Guggenheim Fellowship and a Fulbright Fellowship (to Italy). He is at work on *The Ocean of Clouds* (poems) and *The Perfect Sound: An Autobiography in Stereo* (nonfiction). He teaches at the University of Oregon.

Of "The Bathers, Cassis," Hongo writes: "I spent an early summer month at the Camargo Foundation in Cassis, France, one year, and lived in an apartment overlooking the bay and out toward the Mediterranean Sea. My view was spectacular. Besides the azure waters paradisal, all along one edge of my sight was the imposing, buff-colored bluff of Cap Canaille, to my mind, a kind of Yeatsian Ben Bulben over the entire seascape before me. I say 'buff-colored,' but the truth is it's a chameleon, changing hue and tint under sunlight throughout the day, darkening and sublimely forbidding under rainclouds or at dusk.

"Other constants were noises from the harbor (boat engines and the blaring spiel of tour guides) and occasional shouts from the crowd of sunbathers who occupied the beach and promontory that bordered the Camargo property. But, working at my desk in my studio, I was always inside, away from the bustle and the gleeful sexuality of the throng of bathers. I felt their joyous whoops and screams were an indictment against my own sexual indolence somehow and was reminded of Section XI in Walt Whitman's 'Song of Myself' wherein the poet reflects on 'Twenty-eight young men' who 'bathe by the shore' and a woman who 'owns the fine house by the rise of the bank. . . .'

"It seemed incongruous and profligate for me to be at a desk, doing the fine, mental work of poetry while the scene around me was so vibrant with sensuous splendor. And I imagined myself at twenty, when I surfed and swam most every afternoon in California, when I was once among the bathers myself, reveling in my own body electric, diving into the sea and cutting through waters jeweled in sunlight.

"In a way, the poem is about the life of the mind as it contrasts with the life of the sensuous body, as it then itself becomes the 'unseen hand' that finally retrieves that sensuous body in a moment of imagination."

ISHION HUTCHINSON was born in Port Antonio, Jamaica, in 1983.

Of "Sympathy of a Clear Day," Hutchinson writes: "The poem's setting is Marrakesh, the summer of 2010. But the present is tinged with the colonial/wartime era, specifically with, or via, Winston Churchill's watercolor of the city. His painting is quaint, ochre and pastel. False serenity like a radio turned off: Churchill painted it in January 1943 while on break from the Casablanca conference with Franklin D. Roosevelt, in which they struck the 'unconditional surrender' doctrine, prolonging the war. Nothing of the rage and fury (careless of political sides) appears in his painting. All is mute and dull beneath the imperial gaze. (There is no denying, the poem admits however, the beautiful tonal variants of the sky.) How therefore to look and hear beyond this aesthetico-political silence—the silencing of history—into the present? This question haunts the poem."

DIDI JACKSON was born in Columbus, Ohio, in 1970, and was raised in Florida, where she lived for forty years. The author of the forthcoming collection *Moon Jar* (Red Hen Press, 2020), she teaches creative writing at the University of Vermont.

Jackson writes: "I wrote 'The Burning Bush' immediately after hearing of Brianne's murder. She was my dance student, and we worked closely together for several years. Thanks to social media, I was able to keep in touch with her over time and watch her grow into a beautiful woman who was raising her young son in Central Florida. When the news came that she had been shot by her estranged boyfriend in a murder-suicide, I was devastated, as was our entire community.

"I want more than anything to speak her name, to keep at least her name and her memory alive, and for the world (and the grand audience of *The Best American Poetry*) to know who she was and once again to consider the needless tragedy of gun violence—domestic or otherwise. I want her story, which is the story of so many, to be known.

"'The Burning Bush' contains many dualities, a kind of doublespeak in both language and imagery. My frustration and grief are inconsolable when I think of the possibility of a man's capacity to love and to kill simultaneously, how he can confuse the expressions of passion and murder, veil the communication of beauty and joy and death, and is so often prone to destroy what he cannot control and keep for himself."

MAJOR JACKSON was born in Philadelphia in 1968 and educated at Temple University and the University of Oregon. He is the author of five collections of poetry: *The Absurd Man* (W. W. Norton, 2020), *Roll Deep* (Norton, 2015), *Holding Company* (Norton, 2010), *Hoops* (Norton, 2006), and *Leaving Saturn* (University of Georgia, 2002), which won the Cave Canem Poetry Prize for a first book of poems. He is the editor of The Library of America's *Countee Cullen: Collected Poems* and *Renga for Obama: An Occasional Poem*. He is the poetry editor of the *Harvard Review*.

Of "In Memory of Derek Alton Walcott," Jackson writes: "Unlike many poets of my generation, I never studied with Derek Walcott; still, he was an important influence. Derek modeled a discipline and sensitivity that early on helped me to hear the music beneath the music, the great groundswell and centers of thought and feeling from which his poetry pulses as a distinct sound. In my presence, he generously identified this attribute in Yusef Komunyakaa, another poet whom I also profoundly admire: 'That man is at the center of language, at the center of the song.' I have lived with that utterance echoing in my ears for the better part of two decades. But I have also had to contend with the man off the page.

"Recently I asked an elder poet about Derek Walcott, and he plainly stated, 'Extraordinary poet, regrettably more renowned for his distasteful behavior with women.' Then tacked on: 'I would not let my daughter near him.' In similar discussions with dear friends, women poets who knew Derek early in their lives, a few confirmed, dismissed, then qualified Derek's behavior within the context of his age of rampant and ubiquitous sexism, and yet also quickly added, someone who never sought retribution against women who did not respond to his advances.

"Others who studied with Derek shared unsavory stories that confirmed his reputation. I acknowledged and shared in their pain at being reduced to objects of desire rather than valued primarily for their intelligence and talents.

"This critical ambivalence haunts Walcott's poetry and prodigious legacy as a teacher and writer. Derek's severity as a poet and his moral failings as a man emerge from the same person. So do his lesser-known qualities of generosity and humor, to which I bore witness on several occasions. My writing this elegy allowed me to work through and process my profound gratitude as well as my suppressed anger at a man of enormous complexity, in whom many have found inspiration."

ILYA KAMINSKY was born in Odessa, Ukraine, in 1977, and now lives in Atlanta. He is the author of *Deaf Republic* (Graywolf Press) and *Dancing in Odessa* (Tupelo Press), and coeditor of the *Ecco Anthology of International Poetry* (HarperCollins).

Of "from 'Last Will and Testament,'" Kaminsky writes: "I wanted to write a very brief 'good-bye' lyric. It was going to be a short poem of the last moment that (somehow) refuses grief. But that brief poem refused to end—it kept going. It is still going, somewhere. One day I will catch up with it."

RUTH ELLEN KOCHER was born in 1965 in Wilkes-Barre, Pennsylvania. She is the author of seven books of poetry, including *Third Voice* (Tupelo Press, 2016), *Ending in Planes*, winner of the Noemi Poetry Prize, *Goodbye Lyric: The Gigans and Lovely Gun* (The Sheep Meadow Press, 2014), and *domina Un/blued* (Tupelo Press, 2013). Her poems have been translated into Persian in the Iranian literary magazine *She'r*. She has received grants and fellowships from the National Endowment for the Arts, Yaddo, and Cave Canem. She is the current divisional dean for arts and humanities at the University of Colorado at Boulder.

Of "We May No Longer Consider the End," Kocher writes: "I'm working on a book that recalls my life as a black girl in a working-class white family and in some tough neighborhoods. I've been trying to articulate how my white father understood my anger and helped me to weaponize it as a way to survive in a world he knew could be cruel. He knew what I was up against, as a white man in a white man's world. He wanted to raise 'a young lady' but also made sure that I could fight, and win. This, I think of as a triumph. There is no greater male privilege than the privilege to express anger and so he gave me permission to expect any male privilege, any white privilege, was equally mine."

DEBORAH LANDAU was born in Denver, Colorado. Her books include *Soft Targets*, *The Uses of the Body*, *The Last Usable Hour*, and *Orchidelirium*. In 2016 she was awarded a Guggenheim Fellowship. She teaches in and directs the creative writing program at New York University and lives in Brooklyn with her family.

Of "Soft Targets," Landau writes: "I spend six weeks each year in Paris (directing NYU's writing programs there) and began writing these poems during the string of recent terror attacks in France. It was an intense and frightening time, and the sequence grew into my fourth book, *Soft Targets*, which considers a world beset by political tumult, gun violence, terror attacks, and climate change. I've always written about the vulnerabilities of the body, but here the fear of annihilation extends beyond the self to an imperiled planet on which we are all 'soft targets.'

"The last three lines of the second section of this poem are from 'Frenchman Plotting "Imminent" Attack Is Charged With Terrorism' (*The New York Times*, March 30, 2016)."

QURAYSH ALI LANSANA was born in 1964 in Enid, Oklahoma. He is the author of eight poetry books, three textbooks, and three children's books; the editor of eight anthologies; and the coauthor of a book of pedagogy. He is an upper school humanities teacher at Holland Hall School. From 2002 to 2011 he was the director of the Gwendolyn Brooks Center for black literature and creative writing at Chicago State University. *Our Difficult Sunlight: A Guide to Poetry, Literacy & Social Justice in Classroom & Community* (with Georgia A. Popoff) was published in March 2011 by Teachers & Writers Collaborative. His most recent books include *the skin of dreams: new & selected poems 1995–2018* (Purple Basement Poetics, 2019); *The Whiskey of Our Discontent: Gwendolyn Brooks as Conscience & Change Agent*, with Georgia A. Popoff (Haymarket Books, 2017); and *Revise the Psalm: Work Celebrating the Writings of Gwendolyn Brooks*, with Sandra Jackson-Opoku (Curbside Splendor, 2017).

Of "Higher Calling," Lansana writes: "While sitting in an aisle seat on a plane from Chicago to the 2016 AWP Conference in Los Angeles, I witnessed a poignant and spectacular kerfuffle. An elderly nun from a Central American nation either didn't understand it was against FAA policy to talk on her mobile phone in flight, or just plain refused to close her flip-phone. Dressed in full habit, with a four-inch cross dangling from her neck, her mellifluous tongue was nonstop. Most passengers in earshot laughed at the young blond flight attendant, who grew more frustrated with every attempt to end her conversation. But he didn't speak either language, Spanish or grace."

LI-YOUNG LEE was born in Jakarta, Indonesia, in 1957.

Of "The Undressing," Lee writes: "The poem enacts a dialogue between a time-bound, desire-entangled, foolish, disoriented mortal man with that orienting Goddess Sophia."

DAVID LEHMAN was born in New York City in 1948. Two books were published in 2019: *Playlist*, a poem written in daily increments (University of Pittsburgh Press, 2019), and *One Hundred Autobiographies: A Memoir* (Cornell University Press, 2019).

Lehman writes: "Kevin Young suggested that I use 'It Could Happen to You' as the title of my poem. I often write while listening to music, and Rosemary Clooney's great version of the song was playing as I approached the end of my poem. Jimmy Van Heusen (music) and Johnny Burke (lyrics) wrote this standard in 1943. Jo Stafford's rendition made it on the *Billboard* best-seller list a year later. Besides Rosemary Clooney, vocalists who recorded the song include Bing Crosby, Doris Day, Peggy Lee, Anita O'Day, Frank Sinatra, and Sarah Vaughan. Miles Davis mutes his trumpet in an upbeat version that features John Coltrane on tenor sax. Chet Baker's version incorporates both a scat solo and a trumpet solo."

ADA LIMÓN was born in Sonoma, California, in 1976. She is the author of five books of poetry. Her most recent book, *The Carrying*, was released by Milkweed Editions in 2018.

Limón writes: " 'Cannibal Woman' is a poem that explores both the power and the danger of female rage. I am interested in the stories we tell ourselves about who the monsters are and what happens when we look at monsters with more tenderness and empathy."

REBECCA LINDENBERG was born in Minneapolis in 1978 and grew up in the San Francisco Bay Area. She is the author of *Love, an Index* (McSweeney's, 2012) and *The Logan Notebooks* (Mountain West Poetry Series, 2014). She teaches creative writing at the University of Cincinnati and in the low-residency MFA program at Queens University, and is the poetry editor of *The Cincinnati Review*.

Of "A Brief History of the Future Apocalypse," Lindenberg writes: "I've been hearing the term 'apocalypse' a lot lately—zombie apocalypse, dystopian apocalypse novel, postapocalyptic landscape, etc. Lately I've been hearing it more and more in the context of sociopolitical issues. I find I have a complicated response to all this, because my understanding tells me that what we mean by 'apocalypse,' like 'drastic, cataclysmic event' or 'tyrannical regime change' or 'massive-scale sudden transformation' or generally speaking a disruption of the status quo, is less a futuristic science fiction premise and more of a historical (and in some cases, current cultural/geographical/demographical) fact. But in the ancient meaning of the word, which is also a sort of William Blakean understanding of the word, apocalypse doesn't just mean chaos and destruction. It means revelation, renewal, transformation. I think I wrote this poem to try to remind myself of that—that deep personal grief can be followed by love, that war and cultural conflict can be followed by peace, that in the loam left by a catastrophic volcanic explosion, the best tomatoes grow. But also, crucially, that we have a role in that—to be open to love, to win the peace and equality and liberty for ourselves and our fellows, to plant the tomatoes where the volcano used to be. I wanted to remind myself that it might not be okay, but then again, as much as it is in human nature to ruin things, it is in our nature to care-take and remake them, too. Poetry is one of the ways we do so."

NABILA LOVELACE, a Queens native, was born in 1991; her people hail from Trinidad & Nigeria. *Sons of Achilles*, her debut book of poems, is out now from YesYes Books. You can currently find her kicking it in Tuscaloosa.

Of "The S in 'I Loves You, Porgy,'" Lovelace writes: "There are times when I'm listening to music that I go into a trance because of the voice of the singer. Nina Simone does that to me every time. After listening to her rendition of 'I Loves You, Porgy' upward of a hundred times I could not stop hearing the 's.' I could not hear love without hearing the plural."

CLARENCE MAJOR, born in Atlanta, Georgia, in 1936, is a poet, painter, and novelist. His most recent book of poems, *My Studio*, was published by LSU Press in 2018.

Major writes: "My poem 'Hair' evolved out of my family lore about hair; it also evolved out of my knowledge of superstitions about hair that I found in many other cultures. Early on, I became interested in how the human mind was apparently so easily susceptible to irrational beliefs. I began collecting some of these little 'unbelievable' stories, especially the ones that had no connection with logic or reason or even common sense."

GAIL MAZUR was born in Cambridge, Massachusetts, in 1937. Her collections include *Forbidden City*, *Figures in a Landscape*, *Zeppo's First*

Wife, winner of the Massachusetts Book Prize, and *They Can't Take That Away from Me*. She is founding director of the Blacksmith House Poetry Series in Cambridge. *Land's End: New and Selected Poems* is forthcoming in 2020.

Of "At Land's End," Mazur writes: "Everything in a garden has a history, and in Provincetown, the history of fishing families, artists, and writers is gentled and enriched in their gardens. I often think of Stanley Kunitz, and my 'legacy' anemones, of the order he created in his dune garden, fueled by his sense of agency, of possibility. In this politically devastating time, I'm also companioned by the urgent (and absurd) question: *What are we going to do about Bosnia?* What are we going to do?"

SHANE MCCRAE was born in Portland, Oregon, in 1975. His most recent books are *The Gilded Auction Block* (Farrar, Straus and Giroux, 2019) and *In the Language of My Captor* (Wesleyan University Press, 2017), which won the 2018 Anisfield-Wolf Prize. He has received a Lannan Literary Award, a Whiting Award, and a fellowship from the NEA. He is the poetry editor at *Image*, teaches at Columbia University, and lives in New York City.

Of "The President Visits the Storm," McCrae writes: "Superstitiously, I fear revealing too much about how I write, because I fear that if I do, I won't be able to write at all. But there's no way for me to know I've revealed too much until I've already revealed too much, so: Often, before I go to bed, I'll think something like, 'I sure would like to write a poem,' and then try to conjure up a line or two. That's how 'The President Visits the Storm' got started. I thought the thought, and the lines, 'America you're what a turnout great / Crowd a great crowd big smiles America' occurred to me, almost without additional conjuring beyond the initial thought. Then I went to sleep. The next day, after taking my youngest daughter to school, I opened up gmail—I had written the lines down, as I always do when writing lines down before bed, in a fresh email draft—took a look at the lines, and wrote the rest of the poem. It came out fairly quickly—probably because I had already written some poems about Trump, and knew pretty much the voice I wanted, but also probably because, as John Lydon said, 'anger is an energy.'

"As I wrote the above paragraph, I felt certain I would end it by saying something more about Trump. And while invoking Public Image

Ltd's anti-apartheid anthem, 'Rise,' *is* saying something more about Trump, I had felt I would say something more direct than that. But I find that Trump has wormed his way into an area of evil few people before him have reached, and it is an area beyond the boundaries of effective criticism: What critique can one make of the antichrist? So I will conclude, instead, by saying that I wrote the poem against him, as all art is made against people like him."

JEFFREY MCDANIEL was born in Philadelphia in 1967 and is the author of five books of poetry, most recently *Chapel of Inadvertent Joy* (University of Pittsburgh Press). He is working on a new book, *Holiday in the Islands of Grief,* and has just finished a semiautobiographical novel, *4,000 a.m.* He teaches at Sarah Lawrence College and lives in the Hudson Valley with his twelve-year-old daughter, Camilla, and his wife, Christine Caballero.

Of "Bio from a Parallel World," McDaniel writes: "Right before he died in 1979, my grandfather wanted to change his will and leave every dime he had to me. My father and grandmother talked him out of it. This poem borrows the format of bio writing and imagines the potential burden of that inheritance, as well as possible outcomes of my life if I didn't get clean and sober in 1994."

CAMPBELL MCGRATH was born in Chicago in 1962. For the last twenty-five years he has lived in Miami and taught at Florida International University, where he is the Philip and Patricia Frost Professor of creative writing.

McGrath writes: " 'Miles Davis: Birth of the Cool/The Founding of Brasilia (1950)' was originally intended to be part of my 2016 collection *XX: Poems for the Twentieth Century,* but ended up, somewhat quixotically, on the cutting-room floor. *XX* features a poem for each year of the century, written in various historical guises and personae, and I had two or even three poems for some years, and no very good ideas for others. For 1950 I wanted to write a poem about Miles Davis but I also wanted to commemorate the founding of Brasilia, a purpose-built modernist capital in the wilderness. In the end, I decided that Miles could birth the cool and found Brasilia with his horn, but the poem never felt perfectly finished, and I ended up using a poem about Charlie Parker instead. Two years later I 'rediscovered' the poem, realized it was quite interesting, and wondered why exactly I had failed to find a home for it in *XX*. Oh well, live and learn. I am glad to have it in the world now, even at some remove from the grand historical project that was its genesis, and delighted by its inclusion among such esteemed company."

ANGE MLINKO was born in Philadelphia, Pennsylvania, in 1969. She has lived and worked in New England, New York, Houston, Morocco, and Lebanon, and now teaches in the creative writing program of the University of Florida. She is the author of five collections of poetry, most recently *Distant Mandate* (Farrar, Straus and Giroux, 2017), and her poetry criticism appears regularly in *Poetry*, *London Review of Books*, and *The New York Review of Books*.

Mlinko writes: " 'Sleepwalking in Venice' is one of a series of poems I have been writing from Airbnbs during periods (summers, holidays) when my sons are with their father. I have complete faith in a kind of Rilkean quietism, where the discipline of writing stanzas confers grace in solitude. This poem owes a debt to Joseph Brodsky's book on Venice, *Watermark*, as well as to his Venetian poems; to *Venice: A Traveller's Reader* by John Julius Norwich; to Leopardi and Thomas Mann; and to insomnia."

KAMILAH AISHA MOON was born in Nashville, Tennessee, in 1973. She is the author of *Starshine & Clay* (2017) and *She Has a Name* (2013), both published by Four Way Books. She teaches at Agnes Scott College in Decatur, Georgia.

Of "Fannie Lou Hamer," Moon writes: "This poem was written to move past a moment that hurt deeply and stopped me in my tracks—a scenario that I know I will continue to encounter as our country continues to struggle with closing the chasm between our ideals and our connected realities. This was a weary moment in the long trudge toward the unlimited collective potential we have if enough of us are willing to do the internal and external work necessary for progress."

ANDREW MOTION was born in London in 1952. Cofounder of the Poetry Archive (poetryarchive.org), he was Poet Laureate of the United Kingdom from 1999 to 2009. In 2015 he moved to Baltimore, where he teaches in the writing seminars at Johns Hopkins University. His most recent publication is *Essex Clay* (Faber & Faber, 2018).

Of "The Last of England," Motion writes: "I began writing this poem shortly after leaving London to live in Baltimore in the summer of 2015—and (despite its brevity) took about a year to finish it. The title comes from the famous oil painting of the same name painted by Ford Madox Brown in 1855—which shows two anxious-looking emigrants leaving home to start a new life (in Australia, in fact, and not the USA). My own feelings on leaving the place that had been my home for the previous sixty-two years—or some of them, anyway—are the subject of my poem."

PAUL MULDOON was born in Northern Ireland in 1951. His thirteenth collection of poems, *Frolic and Detour*, was published by Farrar, Straus and Giroux in 2019. He was guest editor of *The Best American Poetry 2005*.

Of "Aubade," Muldoon writes: "The 'dawn song,' known as an aubade or alba, has been a staple of poetry in English since at least the seventeenth century. In this case, the setting is North America in the twenty-first century, though some of the imagery of the poem harks back to the Mongolian shamanic tradition of the 'deer stone' while at least two words have an Irish or Scottish resonance. A haggard is 'an enclosure on a farm for stacking grain, hay, etc.' while a hag refers to the last sheaf of a harvest, thought in many European countries to embody 'the spirit of the corn.'"

JOHN MURILLO was born in Upland, California, in 1971. He is the author of the poetry collections *Up Jump the Boogie* (Cypher Books, 2010) and *Kontemporary Amerikan Poetry* (Four Way Books, 2020). He is an assistant professor of English at Wesleyan University and teaches in the low-residency MFA program at Sierra Nevada College.

NAOMI SHIHAB NYE was born in St. Louis, Missouri, in 1952. Her most recent books are *Voices in the Air: Poems for Listeners* (Greenwillow Books, 2018), and *The Tiny Journalist* (BOA Editions, 2019). She is currently on the faculty of Texas State University.

Of "You Are Your Own State Department," Nye writes: "I am fascinated with how poets attempt to comfort themselves during particularly difficult times—what images, curiosities, connections, and questions arise. Sometimes the audience at a reading feels so supple and hopeful it breaks my heart.

"It's as if people think the poet might put things back in place. This is a tenderness beyond measure—a belief in the powers of language and metaphor—a dream of abiding meaning."

SHARON OLDS was born in San Francisco in 1942 and educated at Stanford University and Columbia University. *Stag's Leap*, her 2012 collection, won both the Pulitzer Prize and England's T. S. Eliot Prize. She is the author of ten previous books of poetry. Her latest book is *Odes* (Alfred A. Knopf, 2016). She teaches creative writing at New York University and helped to found the NYU workshop program for residents of Goldwater Hospital on Roosevelt Island and for veterans of Iraq and Afghanistan. Her next collection, *Arias*, will come out with Knopf in 2019. She lives in New York City.

Of "Rasputin Aria," Olds writes: "I don't remember where I first read about Rasputin—maybe in the Canadian Book of World Records. I was horrified by his cruelty, and by the cruelty done to him. And I felt I had no ability to imagine him from within. So I could almost not even wonder if it changed—his sense of what cruelty was—when he became the subject of it. I seemed to have no way to think about him, yet I was haunted by the terrible humanness of his actions. I think I thought it might be wrong of me to have any sympathy for him. If he had tortured to death someone I knew, would I have wanted to torture him to death, instead of lock him up for life? The facts of his life and death would suddenly shoot through my mind. I knew something of my own schadenfreude, but this was in a realm far more horrible.

"I knew that an eye for an eye, and a tooth for a tooth, meant no *more* than an eye for an eye—not two eyes and a nose. (I looked it up. The talionic law—mirror law—originated with the Babylonian King Hammurabi; later, when the Hebrew Bible came out, Hammurabi's Code was featured in Exodus, Leviticus, and Deuteronomy.) But the murderous, nullifying crimes of rape and castration should not, I thought, be met with rape and castration. Someone somehow would have to stop the retaliation—and the escalation—if our species were to survive. Prison without parole? Eye for an eye seems not promising in terms of the survival of our species or of the earth. To call the original taking of the eye illegal, and the government's taking, in return, of an eye, legal, does not augur well.

"It was months—a year—before it occurred to me to mull over the subject in a poem. Before then, the idea of working in the realm of a poem-draft hadn't occurred to me—I'd been blocked in my thinking.

My pity and terror about the pain the body goes through—'even' the body of a hideously sick, an evil, person—might have been connected (I had not thought of this until now) with my guilt, as a child, for the fact that my sins had tortured Jesus to death. But now I began to somehow trust that I wasn't obsessed in an evil way, but haunted in a normal way by evil and suffering and the uses of power. And then the first line of 'Rasputin Aria,' banal and true, came, and the unscrolling of the poem began. And during the writing of the aria (late 2016), my themes came home to roost—came home to the United States, came home to a certain crock of shit-ka-doodle-do.

"Today I tried to think more about my relationship to the poem since I wrote it. I liked the dysphoria of *rasp* and *sputum* against the melodic word *aria*—like audible sarcasm about human nature. (Often I think about beauty as a problem in art that tries not to look away from the popular human phenomenon of torture. I was saying to someone today, Poetry is a place where torture can be considered while being mourned and protested—art might be a place that provides some moral ground from which to consider it. Maybe it's similar to the fact that we turn to rhyme and meter for their seeming power at times of death and birth.)

"So I was relieved that I'd been able to think about such a person, an egomaniac torture-murderer, and relieved to believe that it was okay for me, in an attempt at a work of art (a first draft no one will ever see) to say, 'I wish I didn't think about him so much.'

"'Rasputin Aria' was written sometime shortly after November 8, 2016. By the end of writing the poem, which came out pretty fast and pretty much whole, I had a better idea of why I'd been obsessed with Rasputin and other dictators. Doing the thinking a poem does seemed to be a kind of action. Obsessing hadn't been action—but being able at last to turn, and face the subject, and take up a pen, was. Most of the poems I write, no one sees—they aren't good enough. So I am used to writing bad poems. The unlikelihood that I am 'up to' writing a good enough poem on a subject doesn't stop me from trying. I joined my first picket line when I was fourteen, but I've been late in believing that I have any ability to exercise any power in art. But I *know* that writing is action, *reading* is action, which can lead to more action in art, and on the street, with our feet, and our voices. In opposition to bullying—to *take the action of speaking up.*

"The sentence above was the way I ended this little essay. And then a couple of further, contradictory thoughts came to me. How was it possible no one had written a poem on the subject of Rasputin? And: no wonder no one has, what a terrible subject. It would need someone smart, nice, tasteful, subtle.

"I'd been called a practitioner of 'sensationalism'—that didn't sound good! And I was a fearful person, anxious, subject to nightmare and hypnopompic 'waking terrors' in childhood, adolescence, and my twenties. Maybe only a really 'Good' person should think about evil.

"Then a friend, the poet Madeleine Mori, read me an Alexander Chee quote, from a Q&A he did with Goodreads in 2016, that allowed me to ask myself helpful questions. What had made me feel ill-equipped to consider Rasputin?

"These were Chee's words: 'For me, writer's block means I've somehow rejected my own ideas as improbable, or unacceptable, or otherwise unthinkable. And so to deal with it I have to deal with why that is. Like many people, I have the belief that keeping myself silent in certain situations will make me invisible or will somehow protect me. When I want to silence myself, I fear myself. So I move toward the block that way: what do I fear will happen if I write this? Is that an honest fear or a dishonest one? The problem with having an imagination is that you can scare yourself out of your whole life if you're not careful. You can imagine a story, or . . . imagine yourself as a failure—both are stories, only one [will be published, and reach another person]. The other is you, blocking the door to your own life.'"

MICHAEL PALMER was born in Manhattan in 1943 and has lived in San Francisco since 1969. His most recent book of poems is *The Laughter of the Sphinx* (New Directions, 2016). He has taught at numerous universities in the United States, Europe, and Asia, and has published translations from a variety of languages, in particular French, Brazilian Portuguese, and Russian. He has also been an artistic collaborator with the Margaret Jenkins Dance Company for more than forty years.

Of "Nord-Sud," Palmer writes: "Now close to two years ago, the French poet and translator Jean Daive asked me to contribute to a colloquium at the Centre International de Poésie in Marseilles celebrating the work of the remarkable and singular poet Pierre Reverdy. This poem resulted. In 1917, Reverdy founded the experimental literary review *Nord-Sud* (*North-South*) with fellow poets Vicente Huidobro, Max Jacob, and Guillaume Apollinaire. His 'north' here becomes

Paris, his 'south' Rome, both cities where I had recently spent time among rivers and butterflies. In 1926, Reverdy burned many of his manuscripts before a group of friends by the Seine."

MORGAN PARKER was born in California in 1987. She is the author of the poetry collections *Magical Negro*, *There Are More Beautiful Things Than Beyoncé*, and *Other People's Comfort Keeps Me Up at Night*. Her debut young adult novel *Who Put This Song On?* will be published in September 2019 by Delacorte Press, and her first book of nonfiction is forthcoming from One World/Random House. She lives in Los Angeles.

Of "The Black Saint & The Sinner Lady & The Dead & The Truth," Parker writes: "I began this poem during a residency at Denniston Hill in June 2017."

WILLIE PERDOMO, born in New York City in 1967, is the author of *The Crazy Bunch*, *The Essential Hits of Shorty Bon Bon*, *Smoking Lovely*, which received the PEN/Open Book Award, and *Where a Nickel Costs a Dime*. He teaches at Phillips Exeter Academy.

Perdomo writes: " 'Head Crack Head Crack'—originally titled 'Crazy Bunch Couplets'—was inspired by 'Two Words,' a hip-hop song written by Kanye West, featuring Yasiin Bey (aka Mos Def), Freeway, and the Boys Choir of Harlem. I started the poem at First Wave @ University of Wisconsin-Madison, where I facilitated a workshop using 'Two Words' as a model. 'Head crack' has an obvious literal meaning. You can hear a verse that is so bangin' that, as Emily Dickinson would have it, it makes you feel physically as if the top of your head were taken off. But 'head crack' is also gambling parlance. In the three-dice game, Cee-Lo, 'head crack' is a trump roll, a 4-5-6, a roll that usually breaks the bank. The rhythm of the poem is in tune with the song it was inspired by. The content of the poem is informed by a crew's trajectory. The crew was called 'The Crazy Bunch,' which became the title of my fourth collection in which the poem was included. I like to think that this poem would have made for solid #bars were I invited to get in on 'Two Words.' Peace."

CARL PHILLIPS was born in Everett, Washington, in 1959. His new chapbook is *Star Map with Action Figures* (Sibling Rivalry Press, 2019), and his new book of poems, *Pale Colors in a Tall Field*, will be out in

2020 from Farrar, Straus and Giroux. He teaches at Washington University in St. Louis.

Of "Star Map with Action Figures," Phillips writes: "I got lost, a little bit, last summer. I can't say, anymore, how this poem came about, exactly, but it seems to me now a way in which I mapped my way forward out of one of desire's many conundrums to a point of recognizing a future beyond conundrum. As the poem suggests, many have fallen on the field of intimacy. Fallen doesn't have to mean it's over, though—hence the open-endedness with which the poem closes; who can say what's next? Disaster, maybe. But joy, too, is possible."

ISHMAEL REED was born in Chattanooga, Tennessee, in 1938. He is the author of more than thirty books to date, including his eleventh novel, *Conjugating Hindi* (Dalkey Archive Press, 2018); his eleventh nonfiction work, *The Complete Muhammad Ali* (Baraka Books, 2015); and *New and Collected Poems, 1964–2007* (Carroll & Graf, 2007). New York's Nuyorican Poets Café presented a staged reading of his play, *The Haunting of Lin-Manuel Miranda*, in January 2019. A new essay collection, *Why No Confederate States in Mexico*, appeared from Baraka Books in 2019. After teaching at the University of California, Berkeley, for more than thirty years, he retired in 2005 and is now a distinguished professor at California College of the Arts. He is a MacArthur Fellow. His author website is located at www.ishmaelreedpub.org.

Of "Just Rollin' Along," Reed writes: "My early poetry was influenced by the modernists whom I studied at the University of Buffalo. The poetry was heavy in symbolism and weighty in obscure allusions. In 1963, I joined a group of black writers in a workshop called Umbra. We were brutal with each other. But my poetry became less pretentious. I began to be comfortable with the vernacular language and forms in the work of Langston Hughes, who was responsible for the publication of my first novel. In my second book of poetry, *Conjure*, I included a blues song based upon the legend of Betty and Dupree. Kip Hanrahan sent my poems to some of the leading jazz musicians and composers, among them Taj Mahal, Carla Bley, Allen Toussaint, David Murray, and Steve Swallow. The result was a concert called *Conjure* at the Public Theater in 1982. The Conjure band, which performs my poems and songs, has been traveling to Europe and Japan for thirty years. The last concert was performed at a jazz festival in Sardinia in 2012. Though I still write in a variety of genres, I return to the blues, and I am lucky enough through the efforts of David Murray and Kip Hanrahan to get some of the leading artists to record them, including Cassandra Wilson, Taj Mahal, Bobby Womack, and Macy Gray. 'Just Rollin' Along' is one of the latest. The idea came from a radio show called *Blues by the Bay*, hosted by Tom Mazzolini, broadcast over KPFA in Berkeley. The encounter between L. C. Good Rockin' Robinson and Bonnie and Clyde was recounted on that show."

PAISLEY REKDAL was born in Seattle, Washington, in 1970. She is the author of a book of essays, *The Night My Mother Met Bruce Lee* (Pantheon, 2000, and Vintage Books, 2002); a hybrid-genre memoir entitled *Intimate* (Tupelo Press, 2012); a book-length essay, *The Broken Country* (University of Georgia Press, 2017); and several books of poetry, including *A Crash of Rhinos* (University of Georgia Press, 2000), *Six Girls Without Pants* (Eastern Washington University Press, 2002), and *The Invention of the Kaleidoscope* (University of Pittsburgh Press, 2007). Her latest book of poems, *Nightingale*, is just out from Copper Canyon Press. She has received a Guggenheim Fellowship. She is the editor and founder of the web history archive project, Mapping Salt Lake City (www.mappingslc.org). In May 2017, she was appointed Utah's poet laureate.

Of "Four Marys," Rekdal writes: "I had the great fortune to be granted a residency at Civitella Ranieri in Umbria, where the director, Dana Prescott, would take the residents out on art tours to look at Piero della Francescas. Her lectures were incredibly thought-provoking and detailed: the opening of my poem comes from her observations of the *Madonna del Parto*'s unusual visual framing, which makes the direction of Mary's movements appear so ambiguous. I am eternally grateful for Dana's knowledge, her enthusiasm, and her support for the arts. This poem is for her.

"The information I include about Wollstonecraft and Mary Shelley comes from years of teaching *Frankenstein*. I trained as a medievalist before I turned to poetry, so some aspects of the poem come from my early education. It may interest the reader to know that I don't have any children myself, and have never given birth, but I am getting older and considering the weight of mortality, as I can see half a lifetime both ahead of and behind me now. For me, that's the true heart of the poem: that strange balance we all experience between death and life."

SONIA SANCHEZ was born in Birmingham, Alabama, in 1934. Her books include *Shake Loose My Skin: New and Selected Poems* (Beacon, 1999). *Morning Haiku*, from the same publisher, appeared in 2010. She has written plays and books for children. For many years she taught at Temple University. In 2018, she received the Wallace Stevens Award. She lives in Philadelphia.

Sanchez writes: "'Belly, Buttocks, and Straight Spines' was written as a commission on the occasion of Kenyan artist Wangechi Mutu's exhibition at Drexel University's Leonard Pearlstein Gallery in 2013. The poem is about women who are killed, who are raped and experimented on by doctors; the poem is a thank-you to my dear sister for shedding light in her art on how women are desecrated, how women are killed, how women are mauled, how women are raped and sometimes even fall in love with their accusers, those who misuse them, who abuse and debase them. The poem is a celebration of her art (papier-mâché, photographs, collages, and sculptures) that tells the story of these women in different forms, touching upon themes of beauty and the environment."

NICOLE SANTALUCIA was born in Johnson City, New York, in 1980. She is the author of *Because I Did Not Die* (Bordighera Press, 2015) and *Spoiled Meat* (Headmistress Press, 2018). She teaches at Shippensburg University in Pennsylvania and has taught poetry workshops in the Cumberland County Prison, Shippensburg Public Library, Boys & Girls Club, and nursing homes.

Of "#MeToo," Santalucia writes: "Within my classroom, more than a dozen students wrote about their sexual assault experiences last year and a few bravely spoke publicly about rape during campus events. The weight of each person's story pressed against my chest all year, making this poem bound to happen. An early draft derived from a writing exercise that I did with my students. We often write together in class and it was their stories, their assaults, their pain, their courage that engulfed me. Their voices unified and amplified—the room, me, them, the pages overflowed (talk about a 'spontaneous overflow of powerful feelings'). I finished the poem months later, after slowly unearthing a horrific experience with my high school soccer coach. Once I gained more clarity of the memory I searched online to find the coach, discovering that he really did run for mayor as a Democrat and he really did name his daughter Nicole. By resituating #MeToo, compressing my memories, and by separating object from subject, I reached clarity for a brief moment. This poem is the convergence of many moments, some are mine, some belong to my students and those who trusted me with their stories, and other moments still live in the silent darkness of survivors."

PHILIP SCHULTZ was born in Rochester, New York, in 1945, and is the founder and director of The Writers Studio, a private school for fiction and poetry writing. His books include *The God of Loneliness: Selected and New Poems* (Houghton Mifflin Harcourt, 2010), *Failure* (Harcourt, 2007), which won the 2008 Pulitzer Prize, *The Wherewithal* (W. W. Norton, 2014), and, most recently, *Luxury* (Norton, 2018). Schultz lives in East Hampton, New York, with his wife, the sculptor Monica Banks. Their two sons are Eli and Augie.

Schultz writes: "I wrote 'The Women's March' soon after my wife and I returned from the march in New York City. I was surprised by how quickly it came and how little revision it required, which is seldom the case with me. It was a fraught time and the march offered refuge, an oasis, as cantankerous and all-consuming as it was. We found it hard to move at times, and often felt more like bystanders than participants. I was so moved by the strong-willed faces everywhere I wasn't always certain where I was; at times it seemed a reprisal of all those marches in San Francisco in the sixties, the startled past reawakened, dreamlike and unconscious. I never before felt quite so honored to be included, and that's what this great onslaught of humanity was all about, inclusion, visibility, and being present. The faces of so many resolute women reminded me of my mother, and I tried to imagine what she would make of all this, if she would understand the significance through me, her only child. The image of her only made the event all the more focused, and inspiring. Her immigrant world with all its limitations for women was now being expanded before our very eyes, in every direction and meaning. I began writing the poem on the bus going back home to East Hampton. The poem felt coauthored, as though once again the role I was being assigned was that of bystander to history."

LLOYD SCHWARTZ was born in Brooklyn, New York, in 1941. He is the author of four poetry collections: *These People* (Wesleyan University Press, 1981), *Goodnight, Gracie* (1992), *Cairo Traffic* (2000), and *Little*

Kisses (2017), from the University of Chicago Press. He edited *Elizabeth Bishop and Her Art* (University of Michigan Press, 1983), *Elizabeth Bishop: Poems, Prose, and Letters* (Library of America, 2008), and *Elizabeth Bishop: Prose* (Farrar, Straus and Giroux, 2011). For thirty-five years, he was classical music editor of the *Boston Phoenix* and in 1994 was awarded the Pulitzer Prize for his "skillful and resonant" reviews. He is the longtime commentator on classical music and the arts for NPR's *Fresh Air*. He teaches at the University of Massachusetts Boston.

Of "Vermeer's Pearl," Schwartz writes: "I fell in love with Vermeer when I started taking the subway by myself to visit the great art museums in Manhattan. Moving to Massachusetts for graduate school, I was still a 'T' ride away from another Vermeer. So what I say in this poem is true—I had never lived in a city without a Vermeer. But in 1990, while I was in Brazil giving a series of talks on Elizabeth Bishop for the U.S. Information Agency, the morning after the still-unsolved Gardner Museum heist, I got a phone call from a friend informing me that I no longer lived in a city with a Vermeer. So I take advantage of every possible opportunity to see Vermeers—just in case. In 2013, the Frick Collection had a show of masterpieces on loan from the Mauritshuis in The Hague, in which the most famous (and most mysterious?) of Vermeer's paintings, the *Girl with a Pearl Earring*, had the place of honor. I practically moved in. Spending so much time with that painting triggered all sorts of new thoughts—and new questions—about Vermeer and his uncanny pearls. Those questions eventually led to this poem."

ALAN SHAPIRO was born in Boston in 1952. His new book of poems is *Against Translation* (University of Chicago Press).

Of "Encore," Shapiro writes: "After finishing my recent book *Life Pig*, I told myself I'd pretty much said all I have to say about my mother's dying and the maddeningly complicated person that she was. I was working under the Aristotelean assumption of writing as catharsis, that writing about what pains you can free you from the pain. 'Encore' is about the recognition of the limits of catharsis. No matter how much one writes about some forms of trauma, the trauma remains."

JANE SHORE was born in Newark, New Jersey, in 1947. She is the author of six books of poems. *That Said: New and Selected Poems* was published by Houghton Mifflin Harcourt in 2012. A Guggenheim

Fellow, a Radcliffe Institute Fellow, and a Hodder Fellow at Princeton, she has taught at Harvard (as the Briggs-Copeland Lecturer on English), Sarah Lawrence, Tufts, M.I.T., the University of Washington, and the University of Hawai'i in Manoa. She teaches at the George Washington University and lives in Washington, DC, and in Vermont.

Shore writes: " 'Who Knows One' is based on the eponymous 'Echad Mi Yodea,' 'a traditional cumulative song in Hebrew, sung at the Passover Seder and found in the Haggadah. It enumerates common Jewish motifs and teachings: "Two are the tablets, Three are the fathers, Four are the mothers, Five are the books of the Torah," and so on. It is meant to be fun and humorous, while still imparting important lessons to the children present. Sometimes it is played as a memory game, recited without looking. Sometimes the goal is to recite the entire verse in one breath.'—Wikipedia

"I wanted to write a secular version of 'Echad Mi Yodea,' using numbers drawn from high or popular culture, sayings, idioms, proverbs, etc., while purposely ditching the strictly religious subject matter of the original. Revising my poem over the course of a whole year, as I drifted further away from the original song, I found that a darker subtext (and a distinct voice) began to emerge. I tried to make each of the song's traditional thirteen stanzas its own little cohesive poem, while at the same time disrupting it with oddball, unpredictable lines. Unlike the original, where each 'number/line' is repeated in its entirety, and without variations, I wanted *only* my refrain lines to repeat. My brain is wired for grids, quilts, repeating images, sequences, all of which give me much pleasure. I am terrible at math."

TRACY K. SMITH was born in Falmouth, Massachusetts, in 1972. She received the 2012 Pulitzer Prize for her collection *Life on Mars* (Graywolf Press), and served as the twenty-second Poet Laureate of the United States from 2017 to 2019.

Smith writes: " 'The Greatest Personal Privation' is an erasure poem and an act of willful listening. The text is drawn from letters sent between members of the Charles Colcock Jones family, but I was listening against the grain, hoping to decipher or imagine the voices of the people enslaved to the Jones family. I imagine that the speaker of my poem is Patience, Phoebe, or one of the other enslaved people whose name has been lost to history."

A. E. STALLINGS, born in 1968, grew up in Decatur, Georgia, and studied classics at the University of Georgia and Oxford University. Her fourth collection of poems, *Like*, was published by Farrar, Straus and Giroux in 2018, and a new verse translation of Hesiod's *Works and Days* appeared from Penguin Classics (2018). She lives with her husband, the journalist John Psaropoulos, and their children, Jason and Atalanta, in Athens, Greece.

Stallings writes: " 'Harm's Way' very much came about as one would expect from the poem's 'it sounds like' opening—contemplating the phrase itself, which suddenly went from an abstraction to an address, in a rural county. 'Harm' could very well be a surname in that neck of the woods, with a road once attached to that family's property. From there, the poem easily led to other dangerous ways, roads, highways, and paths. (Perhaps that I have a teenager very keen to start driving is not irrelevant.)

"This feels to me like a song—even a country song. I think the form is partly influenced by song meters (here I've got trimeters with the odd tetrameter filling out the ghost beats that trimeters tend to call forth), and partly I think by the first six lines of ottava rima, where you have to push through to get three iterations on each rhyme. (I have been writing some longer poems in ottava rima, so I think that pattern started to get under my skin.) But I gave myself the freedom to rhyme only on the even lines.

"In terms of influence, it now occurs to me it might be distantly related to Kipling's delightfully spooky 'The Way Through the Woods.'

"I remember having some qualms in revision about whether the fairy-tale path belonged with these other roads and paths, and trying to take that stanza out and putting it back in, but in the end I think all the ways are on the same map."

ARTHUR SZE was born in New York City in 1950. He has published ten books of poetry, including *Sight Lines* (2019), *Compass Rose* (2014), and *The Ginkgo Light* (2009), all from Copper Canyon Press. A professor emeritus at the Institute of American Indian Arts, he lives in Santa Fe, New Mexico.

Sze writes: " 'The White Orchard' is situated outside our house in Santa Fe and moves through space and time. The structure of the poem follows an invented form: each line picks up a word, or words, from the previous line, and a word from the last line is picked up in the title, so the motion of the poem embodies line and circle."

NATASHA TRETHEWEY was born in Gulfport, Mississippi, in 1966. She is the author of five collections of poetry: *Domestic Work* (2000), *Bellocq's Ophelia* (2002), *Native Guard* (2006)—for which she was awarded the 2007 Pulitzer Prize—*Thrall* (2012), and, most recently, *Monument: Poems New and Selected* (2018). A fellow of the American Academy of Arts and Sciences, she served two terms as the nineteenth Poet Laureate of the United States (2012–2014) and was named a chancellor of the Academy of American Poets in 2019. She is Board of Trustees Professor of English at Northwestern University. She was guest editor of *The Best American Poetry 2017*.

OCEAN VUONG was born in Saigon, Vietnam, in 1988. He is the author of the debut novel *On Earth We're Briefly Gorgeous* (Penguin Press, 2019). His poetry collection *Night Sky with Exit Wounds* won the T. S. Eliot Prize, the Whiting Award, the Thom Gunn Award, and the Forward Prize for Best First Collection. He lives in Northampton, Massachusetts, and teaches in the MFA program at UMass Amherst.

DAVID WOJAHN was born in St. Paul, Minnesota, in 1953. His most recent books are the poetry collection *For the Scribe*, which appeared from the University of Pittsburgh Press in 2017, and *From the Valley of Making: Essays on Contemporary Poetry* (University of Michigan Press, 2015). He teaches at Virginia Commonwealth University and in the MFA program of Vermont College of Fine Arts.

Of "Still Life: Stevens's Wallet on a Key West Hotel Dresser," Wojahn writes: "I love the poetry of Wallace Stevens, but its art-for-art's-sake grandiosity appalls me. His verse has little sense of social consciousness and tells us next to nothing about his domestic life; he famously said that 'money is a kind of poetry.' I wanted to write a poem that both praised and condemned Stevens. To do so I tried to imagine the contents of his wallet, and I placed his wallet on a hotel dresser in Key West, Florida, his annual vacation spot, where he would go to escape his wife, his daughter, and his job as an insurance executive. It was a place where he could drink and make bets on the greyhound races. But even Stevens couldn't escape the real world entirely.

"The Bonus Army, comprised of destitute World War I veterans, marched on Herbert Hoover's Washington in 1932, asking for compensation for their war service. They never received it. General

Douglas MacArthur, whose troops teargassed and dispersed the Bonus Army, killing several of its members in the process, saw to that."

KEVIN YOUNG was born in 1970. He is the author of thirteen books of poetry and nonfiction, most recently *Brown: Poems* (Alfred A. Knopf, 2018) and *Bunk: The Rise of Hoaxes, Humbug, Plagiarists, Phonies, Post-Facts, and Fake News* (Graywolf Press, 2017), both *New York Times* Notable Books. *Bunk* won the Anisfield-Wolf Prize in Nonfiction. His other books include *Blue Laws: Selected & Uncollected Poems 1995–2015* (Knopf, 2016) and *Book of Hours* (Knopf, 2014), which won the Lenore Marshall Prize for poetry from the Academy of American Poets. Young, who was guest editor of *The Best American Poetry 2011*, has edited eight other collections, including *The Collected Poems of Lucille Clifton 1965–2010*. Named University Distinguished Professor at Emory University, Young was inducted into the American Academy of Arts and Sciences in 2016. He is the director of the Schomburg Center for Research in Black Culture and the poetry editor of *The New Yorker*.

Young writes: "The note accompanying the poem's first appearance still stands: 'Hive' is the final poem in my new book *Brown*—a collection that takes up boyhood and brownness, moving through Kansas and the South, from James Brown to John Brown to the *Brown v. Board of Education of Topeka* case that transformed American life. Indeed, life hums here, in this boy remembered or imagined, the poem offering a kind of winged benediction—a song that summons suffering, but does not succumb, I hope. Readers might be interested to know that up until the last moment, I considered cutting the poem from my book—from fears of its being too benedictory—but now I see that it was almost too harrowing yet hopeful. I'm glad I kept it."

The Academy of American Poets Poem-a-Day, eds. Dawn Lundy Martin (February), Tracy K. Smith (April), Matthew Shenoda (May), Rigoberto González (September), and Ross Gay (October). www.poets.org

AGNI, poetry eds. Sumita Chakraborty and Lynne Potts. www .agnionline.bu.edu

The American Poetry Review, ed. Elizabeth Scanlon. www.aprweb.org

The American Scholar, poetry ed. Langdon Hammer.www.theamerican scholar.org

Asheville Poetry Review, eds. Keith Flynn and Luke Hankins. www.ashe villepoetryreview.com

Asian American Literary Review, editors-in-chief Lawrence-Minh Bùi Davis and Gerald Maa. www.aalrmag.org

The Believer, poetry ed. Jericho Brown. www.believermag.com

Black Renaissance Noire, ed. Quincy Troupe. www.nyubrn.org

The Brooklyn Rail, poetry ed. Anselm Berrigan. www.brooklynrail.org

The Cincinnati Review, poetry ed. Rebecca Lindenberg. www.cincinnati review.com

The Common, poetry ed. John Hennessy. www.thecommononline .org

Fifth Wednesday, www.fifthwednesdayjournal.com

Five Points, eds. David Bottoms, Megan Sexton, and Beth Gylys. www .fivepoints.gsu.edu

Freeman's, ed. John Freeman. www.freemansbiannual.com

Green Mountains Review, poetry ed. Elizabeth Powell. www.green mountainsreview.com

Gulf Coast, poetry eds. Michelle Orsi, Theodora Bishop, and Devereux Fortuna. www.gulfcoastmag.org

Harper's, poetry ed. Ben Lerner. www.harpers.org

Harvard Review, poetry ed. Major Jackson. www.harvardreview.org

The Hopkins Review, ed. David Yezzi. www.hopkinsreview.jhu.edu

The Iowa Review, poetry ed. Izzy Casey. www.iowareview.org

The Kenyon Review, poetry ed. David Baker. www.kenyonreview.org

Love's Executive Order, ed. Matthew Lippman. www.lovesexecutive order.com

Massachusetts Review, poetry eds. Ellen Doré Watson and Deborah Gorlin. www.massreview.org

The Nation, poetry eds. Stephanie Burt and Carmen Giménez Smith. www.thenation.com

New England Review, poetry ed. Rick Barot. www.nereview.com

The New Republic, poetry ed. Cathy Park Hong. www.newrepublic .com

New Letters, editor-in-chief Robert Stewart. www.newletters.org

The New Yorker, poetry ed. Kevin Young. www.newyorker.com

The Paris Review, ed. Emily Nemens, advisory ed. Robyn Creswell, guest poetry ed. Shane McCrae. www.theparisreview.org

Ploughshares, poetry ed. John Skoyles. www.pshares.org

Poetry Daily, editorial director Peter Streckfus. www.poems.com

Prairie Schooner, editor-in-chief Kwame Dawes. www.prairieschooner .unl.edu

The Rumpus, poetry eds. Cortney Lamar Charleston, Carolina Ebeid, and Molly Spencer. www.therumpus.net

Salamander, poetry ed. Valerie Duff-Strautmann. www.salamander mag.org

Salmagundi, editor-in-chief Robert Boyers, executive ed. Peg Boyers. www.salmagundi.skidmore.edu

The Seventh Wave, poetry ed. Christina Shideler. www.theseventh wave.co

Southern Indiana Review, poetry eds. Emily Skaja and Marcus Wicker. www.usi.edu/sir

The Southern Review, poetry ed. Jessica Faust. www.thesouthernreview .org

The Southampton Review, poetry ed. Cornelius Eady. thesouthampton review.com

STAT®REC, publisher John Reed. www.statorec.com

SWWIM, eds. Jen Karetnick and Catherine Esposito Prescott. www .swwim.org

The Threepenny Review, ed. Wendy Lesser. www.threepennyreview .com

Time, www.time.com

Times Literary Supplement, poetry ed. Alan Jenkins. www.the-tls.co.uk

Valley Voices, ed. John Zheng. www.libguides.mvsu.edu/valley-voices

Virginia Quarterly Review, poetry ed. Gregory Pardlo. www.vqronline
.org

ACKNOWLEDGMENTS

The series editor thanks Mark Bibbins for his invaluable assistance. Warm thanks go also to Victoria Chang, Amy Gerstler, Stacey Harwood, Terrance Hayes, Didi Jackson, Thomas Moody, Natasha Trethewey, and Virginia Valenzuela; to Glen Hartley and Lynn Chu of Writers' Representatives; and to Ashley Gilliam, David Stanford Burr, Dan Cuddy, Erich Hobbing, and Rosie Mahorter at Scribner. The poetry editors of the magazines that were our sources deserve our applause—they are the secret heroes of contemporary poetry. Major Jackson is indebted to Ryan Conroy and Anna Gibson for their help.

Grateful acknowledgment is made of the magazines in which these poems first appeared and the magazine editors who selected them. A sincere attempt has been made to locate all copyright holders. Unless otherwise noted, copyright to the poems is held by the individual poets.

Dilruba Ahmed, "Phase One" from *Asian American Literary Review*. Reprinted by permission of the poet.

Rosa Alcalá, "You & the Raw Bullets" from Poem-a-Day. Reprinted by permission of the poet.

Margaret Atwood, "Update on Werewolves" from *Freeman's*. Reprinted by permission of the poet.

Catherine Barnett, "Central Park" from *Human Hours*. © 2018 by Catherine Barnett. Reprinted by permission of The Permissions Company, Inc., on behalf of Graywolf Press. Also appeared in *The American Poetry Review*.

Joshua Bennett, "America Will Be" from *The Nation*. Reprinted by permission of the poet.

Fleda Brown, "Afternoons at the Lake" from *The Southern Review*. Reprinted by permission of the poet.

Sumita Chakraborty, "Essay on Joy" from *The Rumpus*. Reprinted by permission of the poet.

Victoria Chang, "Six Obits" from *The Kenyon Review*. Reprinted by permission of the poet.

by Terrance Hayes. Reprinted by permission of Penguin Random House. Also appeared in *Harvard Review*.

Juan Felipe Herrera, "Roll Under the Waves" from *Love's Executive Order*. Reprinted by permission of the poet.

Edward Hirsch, "Stranger by Night" from *The Kenyon Review*. Reprinted by permission of the poet.

Jane Hirshfield, "Ledger" from *Times Literary Supplement*. Reprinted by permission of the poet.

James Hoch, "Sunflowers" from *The American Poetry Review*. Reprinted by permission of the poet.

Bob Holman, "All Praise Cecil Taylor" from *Black Renaissance Noire*. Reprinted by permission of the poet.

Garrett Hongo, "The Bathers, Cassis" from *The Kenyon Review*. Reprinted by permission of the poet.

Ishion Hutchinson, "Sympathy of a Clear Day" from *Freeman's*. Reprinted by permission of the poet.

Didi Jackson, "The Burning Bush" from *New England Review*. Reprinted by permission of the poet.

Major Jackson, "In Memory of Derek Alton Walcott" from *The Paris Review*. Reprinted by permission of the poet.

Ilya Kaminsky, "from 'Last Will and Testament'" from *The Paris Review*. Reprinted by permission of the poet.

Ruth Ellen Kocher, "We May No Longer Consider the End" from Poem-a-Day. Reprinted by permission of the poet.

Deborah Landau, "Soft Targets" from *Soft Targets*. © 2019 by Deborah Landau. Reprinted by permission of The Permissions Company, Inc., on behalf of Copper Canyon Press. Also appeared in *The American Poetry Review*.

Quraysh Ali Lansana, "Higher Calling" from *Gulf Coast*. Reprinted by permission of the poet.

Li-Young Lee, "The Undressing" from *The American Poetry Review*. Reprinted by permission of the poet.

David Lehman, "It Could Happen to You" from *The New Yorker*. Reprinted by permission of the poet.

Ada Limón, "Cannibal Woman" from *The Carrying*. © 2018 by Ada Limón. Reprinted by permission of Milkweed Editions. Also appeared in *SWWIM*.

Rebecca Lindenberg, "A Brief History of the Future Apocalypse" from *Southern Indiana Review*. Reprinted by permission of the poet.